Islamic Surveys

General Editor

C. HILLENBRAND

Muḥammad's Mecca

HISTORY IN THE QUR'ĀN

W. Montgomery Watt

EDINBURGH UNIVERSITY PRESS

Edinburgh University Press
22 George Square, Edinburgh

Set in Trump Medieval
by Speedspools, Edinburgh, and
printed in Great Britain by
Redwood Burn Limited,
Trowbridge, Wilts

British Cataloguing
in Publication Data
Watt, W. Montgomery
Muḥammad's Mecca
1. Muhammad. *Prophet*
2. Muslims—Saudi
Arabia—Biography
I. Title
297'.63 BP75

ISBN 0 85224 565 3
0 85224 611 0 pbk

Contents

PREFACE vii

I *The Qur'ān as a Historical Source*

1 GENERAL CONSIDERATIONS 1

2 THE DATING OF THE QUR'ĀN 3

II *The Arabian Background*

1 GEOGRAPHY AND HISTORY

A cosmology 5

B land-use and climate 6

C references to historical events 12

2 PRE-ISLAMIC ARABIAN SOCIETY

A the tribal system and the concept of 'protection' 15

B 'the fathers' as bearers of tradition 20

3 RELIGION IN PRE-ISLAMIC ARABIA

A fatalism 26

B paganism 29

C belief in *Allāh* as a 'high god' 31

D the monotheisms 36

4 MECCA BEFORE ISLAM

A the sacredness of Mecca and the Ka'ba 38

B Mecca as a commercial centre 39

C attitudes to wealth 41

D knowledge of Judaism and Christianity 44

III *Muḥammad's Early Life*

1 FAMILY AND MARRIAGE 47

2 THE QUESTION OF LITERACY 51

IV *Muḥammad's Prophetic Experience*

1 THE FIRST THREE YEARS 54
2 THE 'MANNERS' OF REVELATION 60
3 THE COLLECTION AND REVISION OF THE QUR'ĀN 68
4 THE CONCEPTION OF THE PROPHETIC VOCATION 72

V *Muḥammad and the Meccan Pagans*

1 THE ROOTS OF OPPOSITION 81
2 THE FINAL BREAK WITH PAGANISM 85
3 VERBAL ARGUMENTS
A the Last Judgement 94
B Muḥammad's prophethood 95
C the stories of former prophets 98
4 PERSECUTION AND THE HIJRA 100

BIBLIOGRAPHY OF WORKS REFERRED TO IN THE TEXT 107

NOTES 108

INDEX 111

Preface

The purpose of this book is to obtain from the Qur'ān as much historical material as possible for the Meccan period of Muḥammad's career. The religious teaching is considered only in so far as it is relevant to historical matters. I made considerable use of the Qur'ān in *Muhammad at Mecca,* but later realized that much more was to be gained from it, especially about the Arabian background. Since writing *Muhammad at Mecca* I have also become more fully aware of the presence in Mecca of many persons who believed in *Allāh* as a high or supreme deity to whom other deities might make intercession, and I now regard this as a factor of primary importance. The present volume gives an opportunity to reconsider Muḥammad's religious development in the light of this factor. I originally conceived and planned this work to cover the whole of Muḥammad's career, but eventually decided to restrict it to the Meccan period, partly because this by itself provided sufficient material for a book of reasonable size, and partly because it seemed that there would be little to say about the subsequent period that was not already said in *Muhammad at Medina.*

The research for this book began over twenty years ago, when some early chapters were drafted. The material was later used in a number of articles:

'Fathers and Sons in Muḥammad's Arabia', a paper read to the International Association for the History of Religion at Lancaster, August 1975, but not published.

'Pre-Islamic Arabian Religion in the Qur'ān', *Islamic Studies,* xv (1976), 73-9.

'The Arabian Background of the Qur'ān', *Studies in the History of Arabia,* Vol 1, part 1, Riyadh 1979(?). 3-13.

'Qur'ānic References to the Climate of Arabia'. *B. H. Zaidi Felicitation Volume,* ed. Malik Ram, New Delhi 1980, 57-64.

'Pre-Islamic Attitudes to Wealth', *Hakeem Abdul Hameed Felicitation Volume,* New Delhi 1982, 69-75.

The research has been completed and the volume written during the last six or eight months, though it was possible to incorporate parts of the earlier drafts at certain points.

I

The Qur'ān as a Historical Source

I GENERAL CONSIDERATIONS

During the present century various Western scholars have taken the view that the only reliable source for the life and career of Muḥammad is the Qur'ān itself. This view arises in part from earlier criticisms of the reliability of Ḥadīth, coupled with the idea that Ḥadīth constitute the main source for the biography of Muḥammad apart from the Qur'ān. This last idea is completely mistaken, since nearly the whole corpus of Ḥadīth is concerned with legal and theological matters and provides hardly anything of value for the general historian of the career of Muḥammad; only al-Bukhārī has a 'book' on the *Maghāzī* or Expeditions of Muḥammad. What may be called biography- or *Sīra*-material, such as is found in the *Sīra* of Ibn Hishām, is almost completely distinct from Ḥadīth in the strict sense and is little affected by the criticisms of the latter. I have argued elsewhere that, while some of the *Sīra*-material may be criticized on grounds other than those applicable to Ḥadīth, there is a basic core of material which is sound.[1] Not merely does this sound material supplement the Qur'ān, but it would be impossible to make sense of the historical material in the Qur'ān without assuming the truth of this core.

Personally I am convinced that Muḥammad was sincere in believing that what came to him as revelation (*waḥy*) was not the product of conscious thought on his part. I consider that Muḥammad was truly a prophet, and think that we Christians should admit this on the basis of the Christian principle that 'by their fruits you will know them', since through the centuries Islam has produced many upright and saintly people. If he is a prophet, too, then in accordance with the Christian doctrine that the Holy Spirit spoke by the prophets, the Qur'ān may be accepted as of divine origin. In saying this, however, I do not exclude the possibility that God makes his revelations through a person's unconscious mind; and indeed something of this sort seems to be required if we are to explain adequately all the phenomena.

The Qur'ān itself claims that it is 'an Arabic Qur'ān' (12.2; etc.), and this implies not merely that it is in the Arabic language, but that, since it was addressed in the first place to Arabs of the Hijaz, it speaks in terms of their world-picture in all its aspects. This includes even points in which their world-picture was mistaken. From this it would appear to follow that, wherever it was not part of God's purpose to correct such ideas, he spoke to them in terms of these mistaken ideas. They presumably believed that the earth was flat and there are several verses in the Qur'ān which speak of it having been spread out as a wide expanse, which the first hearers would understand as being flat, though later Muslim scholars like al-Bayḍāwī knew that the earth was spherical and that the flatness was only approximate.[2] The same principle applies to mistaken ideas about what Jews and Christians believed, namely, that some people in Mecca wrongly supposed certain beliefs to be held by Jews and Christians, and that it was not essential for God's purpose that false ideas of this sort should be corrected. Examples would be the idea that Christians took Jesus and Mary to be 'two gods apart from God', and that the Jews held 'Uzayr (Ezra) to be the son of God.[3]

It is unlikely, however, that mistakes of this sort will occur in statements about the beliefs and customs of the inhabitants of Mecca and the regions around. In such matters the audience addressed by the Qur'ān was well-informed, and in these respects what is asserted in the Qur'ān may be accepted as true. The same applies to statements about Muḥammad himself and his relations with his followers and opponents. The aim of the present study is to bring together this contemporary or near-contemporary material vouched for by the Qur'ān, using the core or main outline of the Sīra as a framework into which particular details may be fitted.

It has seemed best, on the whole, to translate Qur'ānic passages specially for this book. This makes it possible to select the translation which best brings out the points being illustrated by the quotations. The translation is my own, but I have had before me those in English of Richard Bell and Marmaduke Pickthall (the latter being interleaved with the text of the Qur'ān I was using), and also the German translation of Rudi Paret. I consider the last to be the best European translation in respect of linguistic scholarship, because Paret had systematically and painstakingly compared all the Qur'ānic usages of particular phrases, and this gives his version great authority. The vast amount of work he had done is well seen from his *Kommentar und Konkordanz*, which is an invaluable research tool once one has worked out a method of using it. I have sometimes also consulted the commentaries of aṭ-Ṭabarī, az-Zamakhsharī, al-Bayḍāwī and the Jalālayn, and made use of information about 'occasions of revelation'.

I have normally offered no justification of my choice of rendering for a difficult word or phrase, though some justification will nearly always be found in Paret. In most cases, too, whichever choice is made does not affect the general argument. On the other hand, where Paret aimed at complete clarity regardless of style, I have aimed at the greatest possible succinctness, as best conveying to an English reader the special flavour of the Qur'ān, even if it means leaving him to puzzle out some points; and for the same reason I have divided passages into short lines. The verse-numbering is that of the standard Egyptian edition.

2 THE DATING OF THE QUR'ĀN

For many purposes Western scholars find it desirable to have at least a rough idea of the date at which the various passages of the Qur'ān were revealed. This enables them to study the changes in emphasis in the Qur'ānic message as the community of Muslims grew and came to have new and different needs. For Western scholars it is a truism to see in a religion of today something living and growing and therefore changing or, as they prefer to say, developing. To the Arab of Muḥammad's time change was abhorrent, and what was true was the unchanging. Something of this feeling about change has persisted in Islam, and few Muslims have been ready to think of their religion as something developing.

During the nineteenth century various European scholars, such as Sir William Muir and Hubert Grimme, tried to work out a chronology of the Qur'ān. The most successful was Theodor Nöldeke.[4] Making use of the material provided by the traditional 'occasions of revelation', he observed that the sūras generally regarded as early had very short verses and those regarded as late very long verses. He then propounded the theory that the date at which a sūra was revealed could be roughly determined by the average length of its verses, the short being early, the long late, and those of medium length in the middle period. Muslim scholars had classified the sūras as Meccan or Medinan (that is, after the Hijra), but Nöldeke further divided the Meccan period into three. Within each of the four periods he assigned a specific place to each sūra, so that in effect he rearranged the whole Qur'ān. Nöldeke's dating of the Qur'ān was widely accepted by Western scholars.

Nöldeke, following the practice of Muslim scholars, mostly treated each sūra as a whole, although it was known to him and to them from the 'occasions of revelation' that some verses had been revealed at a different date from the rest of the sūra; for example, a Meccan sūra might contain a few verses revealed at Medina. A completely new approach was adopted by Richard Bell.[5] He accepted the view common among Muslims that the Qur'ān had mostly been revealed in short passages which had then been put together or 'collected' into sūras, either by Muḥammad himself or by the later 'collectors'. His chief concern, however, was to find an explanation for the many different kinds of unevenness in the style of the Qur'ān. He held that many of these were due to the way in which separate passages had been 'collected' or fitted together into sūras, and he further maintained that in the course of the 'collection' by Muḥammad himself there had been some revision of the text, presumably on the basis of further revelation. I believe that the lines of study pioneered by Bell may yet lead to important results.

The latest attempt to give a chronology of the Qur'ān is that of Régis Blachère.[6] He appears to have done most of his work before becoming aware of Bell's theories, doubtless because of the Second World War. In general he follows Nöldeke, but he makes some small readjustments and entirely rearranges Nöldeke's first Meccan period 'by grouping in series the sūras which have a certain basic similarity', and in fact he has four series. In his French translation he places whole sūras in a chronological order (with the exception of 96 and 74, each of which he divides into two), but he frequently notes that a section of a sūra is later than the main part. In so far as a chronological order is needed in this study, I shall mainly follow that of Blachère.

II
The Arabian Background

In the course of proclaiming its religious message the Qur'ān has many phrases and verses which throw light on the conditions familiar both to the people of Mecca and to the nomads of the desert. The present chapter is far from being exhaustive, but presents some of the material relevant to topics of general interest.

1 GEOGRAPHY AND HISTORY

A *cosmology*

It is useful to begin by looking at the cosmological ideas implicit in the Qur'ān, since these reinforce the assertion made in the previous chapter that the Qur'ān, like every religious scripture, addresses its first audience in terms of their own language, their own customs and their general world-view. If the Qur'ān had spoken of the earth going round the sun, even incidentally, that would have been incredible to the Arabs of the time, and would have given opponents an additional reason for rejecting the Qur'ān. Instead it speaks fairly clearly in terms of a flat earth which God has spread out. Several different Arabic words are used, but all would be interpreted by the hearers in terms of their belief that the earth is flat, though of course there is no special emphasis on flatness, since no one supposed the earth could be otherwise. The heaven is thought of as a roof over the earth. Sometimes it is said to have been built, presumably of stone; but a verse which speaks of the mountains as tent-pegs suggests that it may also have been thought of as a bedouin tent. There is also mention of seven heavens. The following is a selection of the many verses in which these ideas are present.[1]

> Are you harder to create or the heaven he built?
> He raised up its roof and ordered it,
> he darkened its night and brought out its morn.
> The earth thereafter he spread out,
> brought from it its water and its pasture,
> and the mountains made fast—
> a provision for you and your herds (79.27–33)

> Will they not regard the camels, how they are formed?
> and the heaven how it is raised?
> and the mountains how they are set up?
> and the earth how it is spread out? (88.17–20)

Did we not make the earth an expanse
and the mountains pegs? (78.6, 7)

The heaven we have built with hands,
and it is we who make it of vast extent;
and the earth we have laid flat,
and good is our spreading. (51.47, 48)

God made for you the earth an expanse
that in it you might travel by pathways and passes.
(71.19, 20)

(My Lord) who made for you the earth a bed,
and strung for you in it pathways . . . (20.53)

(Your Lord) it is who spread out the earth,
and set in it fixed (mountains) and rivers. (13.3)

(Your Lord) made for you the earth a carpet (*firāsh*)
and the heaven an edifice,
and sent down from heaven water
whereby he produced fruits—a provision for you . . . (2.22)

The fact that these passages reflect a cosmology which we now regard as primitive does not detract from their religious message. They proclaim that it is God who created the earth and that he has made it a suitable and convenient place for human beings to live in. The commentator al-Bayḍāwī (d.1258) was well aware of this character of Qur'ānic cosmology but did not find it at all an embarrassment although he himself knew that the earth was spherical.[2]

B *land-use and climate*

Before oil was discovered and Arabs became millionaires the traditional Western idea of an Arab was of nomad living in a tent in the desert; the word 'desert' is loosely used for what is rather steppe. This was never the whole truth about Arabia, for there were towns and oases and fertile regions. There was also much desert, however, and desert conditions form the background of many Qur'ānic passages. Desert experiences lie behind the important metaphorical uses of the words *ḍalāl* (going astray) and *hudā* (guidance). The camel is not merely 'the ship of the desert' but it alone makes life there possible by its ability to absorb liquid from vegetation; so it is not surprising to find a verse (88.17, quoted above) expressing admiration at the wonder of its creation.[3] Most references in the Qur'ān to 'cattle' and 'herds' should probably be understood of camels. One of the marks of the Last Day is that the pregnant camels are neglected (81.4). The hardships of desert life are touched on with a reference to having nothing to eat except dry thorn

(88.6). It is entirely in keeping, too, with the outlook of the desert that Paradise is conceived in the Qur'ān as a garden with rivers running through it. The verse (71.20) quoted above about travelling in the earth by pathways and passes suggests the experiences of merchants' caravans.

It is also remarkable, however, to note that apart from the descriptions of Paradise, there are many references in the Qur'ān to gardens, fruits, herbage and other crops, and to the climatic conditions which produce them and sometimes destroy them. Many of these references occur in passages which call attention to God's power and goodness.

First it may be noticed that many passages describe how God sends water from heaven and how this leads to the growth of plants of many kinds.

Let man consider his food.
We poured out water in showers,
we split the earth open, and caused to grow in it grain
and grapes and clover
and olives and palms
and luxuriant orchards
and fruit and herbage—
an enjoyment for you and your herds. (80.24–32)

He it is who sent down water from heaven.
Thereby we produced every kind of plant;
among them we produced green (shoots),
from which we brought close-packed grain,
and from the spathes of the palms low-hanging date-clusters;
and gardens of grapes and olives and pomegranates—
look, when they bear fruit, how they bear and ripen;
in that are signs for believing people. (6.99)

The rain also supports scrub-vegetation on which animals may pasture:

He it is who sent down water for you from heaven
from which is drink
and from which is scrub for your pasturing;
thereby he makes corn grow for you
and olives and palms and vines and all fruits;
in that is a sign for reflecting people. (16.10f.)

There are similar but shorter passages in 14.32; 23.18–20; 78.14–16. In 79.30f. the bringing of water from the earth suggests a spring, while in 2.71 there is mention of the use of animals to irrigate crops on ploughed land.

The rain is sometimes spoken of as coming to 'dead' earth, and the appearance of vegetation then becomes a sign of the resurrection of human beings.

> We have sent down from heaven blessed water,
> and thereby made gardens to grow
> and grain for harvesting
> and tall palms with densely-fruited spathes—
> a provision for God's servants—
> and thereby we revive dead land.
> Such is the rising (from the tomb). (50.9–11)

> Among his signs is that you see the earth withered,
> then when we sent down water on it, it stirs and swells.
> He who revived it is reviving the dead;
> over everything has he power. (41.39)

This revival of dead earth is also mentioned briefly in 7.57; 16.65; 25.48; 36.33 and 45.5. In 32.27 the earth is described as 'barren' (*juruz*). These descriptions are specially appropriate in lands where there is a long dry summer season when nothing grows.

In addition to these general passages there are also passages which speak of different qualities of land and differential treatment of the owners.

> In the earth are neighbouring portions
> and gardens with vines and corn
> and palms double-stemmed and single,
> (all) irrigated with the same water,
> but we make one (portion) excel another in fruitfulness.
> In that are signs for intelligent people. (13.4)

> He it is who sends the winds with tidings before his mercy,
> until, when they carry heavy clouds,
> we drive them to a dead land,
> and thereby send down water,
> and thereby bring forth of all fruits;
> in this (same) way we bring forth the dead:
> perhaps you will be admonished.
> The good land's crop comes forth by permission of its lord,
> but of that which is bad the crop comes forth only scantily.
> Thus do we change the signs for a thankful people. (7.57f.)

In this latter passage it seems that there is a difference in the quality of the land in the two cases; one is good (*ṭayyib*) and the other is bad (*khabutha*). In the first passage, however, there is no mention of the quality of the land, and it is possible that God causes the difference as recompense for the differing conduct of the individuals concerned. In the following passage it is clearly stated that a difference in respect of 'provision' (*rizq*) is a consequence of a man's own conduct.

When we cause people to experience our mercy,
they rejoice at it;
but if evil strikes them for what their hands have sent forward,
they are in despair.
Have they not seen that for whom he will
God enlarges the provision or restricts it?
In that are signs for believing people. (30.36f.)

It is presumably along this line that one should interpret the statement in 16.71 that 'God has made one superior to another in provision', and perhaps also that in 67.21 about the possibility of his withholding provision.

God's recompensing of men is also connected with another feature of the Arabian climate, namely, the sudden occurrence of natural calamities, especially such as lead to the withering of vegetation. As an example of this 10.24 may be quoted.

The likeness of the present life—
(it is) like water we sent down from heaven;
with it the plants of the earth mingled (and flourished),
those eaten by men and cattle,
until when the earth has put on her finery
and has adorned herself, and her people think
that over her they have power,
our event comes to her by night or day,
and we make her stubble,
as if she had not existed the day before.
Thus we discriminate the signs for reflecting people.

In this case the calamity is a punishment for the people affected, but in others it seems to be just a part of the seasonal changes.

Did you not see that God sent down water from heaven
and channelled it in the earth as springs?
Next he produces by it crops of varied kind;
next it dries up and you see it withered;
next he makes it broken debris—
a reminder in that for the intelligent. (39.21; cf. 18.45)

The same sequence is described in 57.20, but is there linked with the thought of the transience of earthly life.

Know that this present life is play and sport and outward show;
it is emulous boasting with one another
and vying in wealth and children.

It is like a rain-shower
whose vegetation the unbelievers admire;
next it dries up and you see it withered;
next it is broken debris.
In the world to come is severe punishment
and forgiveness from God and approval.
This present life is only enjoyment of delusion.

Other passages, however, suggest that the withering (or yellowing) of vegetation, though a natural occurrence, is a part of God's activity with regard to men.

Have you considered (the fields) you plough?
Do you grow (the grain)
or are we the growers?
Had we willed we had made it broken debris
and you would be left lamenting. (56.63–5)

God it is who sends the winds,
stirring up cloud and spreading it, as he will,
in the heaven, and breaking it up;
you see the fine rain coming from its midst;
and when with it he strikes whom he wills of his servants,
then they rejoice,
though before its descent upon them—
before it they were in despair.
Look then at the outcome of God's mercy,
how he revives the earth after its death.
He is the reviver of the dead; over everything he has power.
If we send wind and they see the crops withered,
they afterwards remain unbelieving. (30.48–51)

Various agents are mentioned as bringing about the destruction of the vegetation. In 22.66 it is 'a fire-bearing whirlwind' (*iʿṣār fī-hi nār*), in 3.117 'a frost-bearing wind' (*rīḥ fī-hi ṣirr*). The possibility of God sending a *ḥāṣib* is mentioned in 67.17, and this is interpreted as a storm raising dust and small stones and could perhaps be rendered 'sandstorm'. Some of these at least would produce the 'yellowing' or 'withering' of plant life already mentioned, and this would lead to the later stage of 'broken debris' (*ḥuṭām*). A slight variant of this is found in 87.4,5, where God 'brought forth the pasture, then made it decaying rubbish'; the word *ghuthā'* here translated 'rubbish' refers specially to the remains of vegetation carried down the wadi by a torrent.

A completely different sort of calamity is described in 2.264f.

O believers, do not make your alms worthless
by claiming merit or injuring,

like him who contributes his wealth to be seen of men,
believing not in God and the Last Day.
His likeness is that of a soil-covered height
which a downpour strikes and leaves bare.
(These men) have no power over aught of what they acquired;
God guides not the unbelieving people.
The likeness of those contributing their wealth
to gain God's approval and establish themselves
is as that of a garden on a fruitful upland,
which, when a downpour strikes it, gives its fruit twofold;
but, if no downpour strikes it, there is dew.
Of what you do God is aware.

The calamity which befalls the unbeliever is clearly soil-erosion as a result of torrential rain (*wābil*) but the precise meaning of some of the terms is uncertain. The word translated 'height', *ṣafwān*, is properly stony or rocky ground which in some way is smooth; and its final state is *ṣald*, which the commentators agree means without plants, though the primary meaning is hard and smooth. The contrast is with a *rabwa* or fruitful upland where heavy rain increases the yield without washing away the soil and where absence of rain is partly replaced by dew.

In the story or parable of the arrogant man with two gardens (18.32–44) the friend mentions two possibilities of calamity (verses 40,41), of which the first is not unlike soil-erosion.

. . . perhaps my Lord
will send upon (your garden) a punishment from heaven,
making it a slippery dune;
or else the water will sink into the ground
where you will not be able to trace it.

The word *ḥusbān* is probably to be taken as the verbal noun with the sense of 'reckoning' or 'calamity sent to settle a reckoning' and so may be translated 'punishment'. Several Muslim commentators preferred 'thunderbolt', and the word can also mean 'hail'; but, while these phenomena occur in Arabia, it is not clear how they could transform the garden into a slippery dune (*ṣaʿīd zalaq*). This last phrase again is not clear. There is agreement that *ṣaʿīd* is a dry height and that the primary meaning of *zalaq* is 'slippery'; but al-Bayḍāwī seems to think that the place is slippery because of thick vegetation. It seems preferably to suppose that the place is slippery because there is no vegetation—even in Britain a sandy or dusty slope can be slippery when there are no tufts of grass on it—and that the 'punishment' is left unspecified. The punishment would then be something which fell or blew on the garden and eroded the soil. The other calamity is probably the drying up of a well (cf. 67.30).

In the story of the greedy and irreligious owners of a garden (68.17–33) the main emphasis is on the fact that they are punished for their lack of true faith, and the calamity is described briefly:

> There went round it one from your Lord while they slept,
> and in the morning it was as if reaped. (verses 19,20)

Some commentators suggest that 'reaped' (*ṣarīm*) should rather be 'black and burnt up', and something like this would in any case be implied. Again in the phrase *ṭāfa . . . ṭā'if* the subject is not necessarily personal, but could, for example, be an unusually hot wind. Thus there is nothing to necessitate supposing that the agent of God's punishment was other than something which occurs naturally in Arabia.

In all this it is to be particularly noted how religious lessons are subtly drawn from familiar climatic phenomena. In Arabian conditions the revival of 'dead' land by rain, after months without any, would be a specially strong argument for the resurrection of human beings.

c *references to historical events*

There are a few references in the Qur'ān to historical events in Arabia in the previous century or so, but none throws much light on what happened.

The earliest is the collapse of the civilization of South Arabia, which is described and placed in a theological setting.

> Sheba had in their habitation a sign,
> two gardens to right and left.
> 'Eat from the provision of your Lord and thank him—
> a good land and a forgiving Lord'.
> But they turned away, and we sent upon them
> the flood of the dam, and changed their two gardens
> into two gardens with bitter fruit
> and tamarisks and some few lote-trees.
> That was our reward for their ingratitude. (34.15–17)

This event is commonly called the breaking of the dam of Ma'rib. Traditionally it was because of this that several Yemenite tribes abandoned settled life, took to the desert and moved northwards. Archaeological evidence suggests that the breakdown of the irrigation works on which the civilization of South Arabia depended was not a single event but occurred in several stages. It also suggests that this was not the cause of the collapse of the civilization but rather its outcome, following on a decline in the trade which was the real source of its livelihood, and on a consequent reduction in the population.[4] The decline in trade is apparently described in the slightly mysterious verses which follow.

> Between them and the towns we had blessed
> we set towns (still) seen,
> and measured the journey between them (to be easy).
> 'Travel in them securely by night and day'.
> But they said, 'O our Lord, lengthen our stages',
> wronging themselves. We made them to be talked of,
> and scattered them widely.
> In that are signs for the patient and thankful. (34.18f.)

The reminiscence of another event is possibly to be found in 85.4–8.

> Cursed be the men of the Trench, the fire with its fuel!
> Over it they are sitting
> as they witness how they are treating the believers;
> they tortured them only because they believed in God.

This has mostly been taken to refer to the persecution of Christians in Najrān by the Jewish king Dhū-Nuwās about 523 AD. Some modern scholars, however, have argued strongly that the Trench or Pit of fire is Hell, and that the men there are Meccan pagans being punished, and witnessing to their crimes against the believers;[5] but there are linguistic difficulties about this interpretation. On the other hand there is impressive support for the older interpretation in a document recently published by Irfan Shahid.[6] This describes how the Jews, after collecting two thousand Christians into a church, 'brought wood and surrounded the church from the outside and threw fire into it and burnt it together with all that was found in it'.

There is a contemporary reference to the 'Romans' (*Rūm*), that is, the Byzantines, in 30.2–4.

> Defeated are the Romans
> in the nearer land, but after their defeat they will defeat (others)
> in a few years; to God belongs the affair before and after,
> and on that day the believers will rejoice.

This is mostly taken to refer to the Persian advance into Syria which led to the capture of Jerusalem in 614. The Meccans would be aware of that series of events because it would affect their trade; and many of them may have had pro-Byzantine sympathies. The passage could then be understood as expressing support for the Byzantines against the party in Mecca which favoured the Persians. This consisted of those who traded mainly with Iraq, and a prominent member of this group, an-Nadr ibn-al-Ḥārith of the clan of ʿAbd-ad-Dār, was an outspoken opponent of the Muslims. Jerusalem was in fact recovered by Heraclius in 624.

A variant text reverses the passive and active verbs, so that the Byzantines are said to have defeated (others) in the past, but are to be defeated in a few years. If this was the original form, then it presumably referred to a Byzantine victory over a Muslim force, such as that at Mu'ta in 630. That date appears to be too late, however, for the revelation of this passage. Nöldeke and Blachère place the sūra in the third Meccan period, and the shortness of verses 2 and 3 suggests that the passage may be even earlier—verses 1 to 5 seem to be separate from the rest of the sūra. What is conceivable is that the second form was preferred to the first by someone other than Muḥammad, perhaps after his death, in order to encourage the Muslims after Mu'ta. There may also have been some interest in showing that a prophecy had been fulfilled. Whatever text and interpretation is adopted, the passage shows that men in Mecca had some knowledge of Byzantine affairs and of their effects on Mecca.

Those of Muḥammad's contemporaries who had made the journey to Damascus had probably seen the ruins of Madā'in Ṣāliḥ or the Settlements of Ṣāliḥ, who, according to the Qur'ān, was the prophet who had been sent to the now extinct tribe of Thamūd. The connection with Thamūd may have been tenuous and the traditional story vague, but at least the Meccans knew that town-dwelling peoples who had once existed had subsequently disappeared. The ruins of Madā'in Ṣāliḥ are referred to briefly in 29.38 and more fully in 27.51f.

> They disbelieved (their prophet),
> and there came upon them the earthquake,
> and in the morning they lay prostrate (and dead) in their dwelling.
> See what was the outcome of their plotting;
> we destroyed them and their people altogether;
> those are their houses ruined because of their wrongdoing.

There were probably several other sites with archaeological remains known to the Meccans, and indeed 29.38 may refer to one of these rather than to Madā'in Ṣāliḥ.

> How many a town have we destroyed in its wickedness,
> now lying in ruins!
> How many a well unused! How many a lofty castle! (22.45)
> How many a town have we destroyed, proud of its good life!
> Those are their dwellings not lived in after them
> save for a little; and we (God) are the inheritors. (28.58)

In all these cases the Qur'ān regards the ruin of the town as having come about because the inhabitants disbelieved their prophet. In many verses unbelievers are urged to 'travel in the land' and see the fate of former unbelievers

> Have (the unbelievers) not travelled in the land
> and seen what the outcome was for those before them
> who were stronger than they and cultivated the earth
> and built on it more than they?
> (Their punishment was for disbelieving God's signs.) (30.9)
>
> Say: Travel in the land and see what was the outcome
> for those who disbelieved (the revelation). (6.11)

Familiarity with ruins is thus made to serve a religious purpose.[7]

The theological interpretation of events is also present in Sūra 105 which speaks of 'them of the Elephant'. This is always taken to refer to an expedition against Mecca about the year 570 by Abraha, the Abyssinian viceroy of the Yemen, when he struck fear into the Arabs by using a fighting elephant. According to the Qur'ān God foiled the plans of the invaders by sending against them great flocks of birds which pelted them with 'stones of baked clay'. This does not tell us much about the expedition except that it failed. What would be interesting to know would be whether, prior to this revelation, there had been any tendency to attribute the deliverance of Mecca to God.

2 PRE-ISLAMIC ARABIAN SOCIETY

The Qur'ān does not describe Arabian society so closely as it describes some current religious views, but various ideas about the nature of society are implicit in many passages. Indeed for an understanding of certain passages it is essential to know something of social concepts and customs.

A *the tribal system and the concept of 'protection'*

The main social unit was the group of kinsmen commonly called tribe or clan. By Muḥammad's time relationship was reckoned mainly in the male line, but there is evidence that somewhat earlier kinship in the female line had been more important, at least in certain parts of Arabia, and notably in Medina.[8] This is referred to in a verse (25.54) which states that God made humanity *nasab* and *ṣihr*. As al-Bayḍāwī notes, *nasab* is relationship in the male line, *ṣihr* in the female; but it is not certain whether this means relationship by marriage or full matrilineal kinship (of which al-Bayḍāwī presumably had no experience). Whatever the precise form of kinship, there was no doubt about who were members of the group. Besides its full members a tribe or clan could have people attached to it in various ways. One such was the status of *jār* or 'protected neighbour' (of which more presently). In the biographical material about Muḥammad there are many references to the 'confederate' or *ḥalīf*, who sometimes lived with the clan, though perhaps not always; but this term does not occur in the Qur'ān. On the other hand the words *walī* and *mawlā* occur frequently (both meaning either 'patron' or 'client'), and could apply to the confederate who was mostly a client. The status of confederate, patron and client was created by a mutual oath, and will be further explained presently.

Also attached to the clan were slaves. If Arabs, they were usually either persons who had been captured in fighting and not ransomed, or children of captured women fathered by some one other than the woman's owner. There were also Abyssinian and other non-Arab slaves. The Qur'ān accepted the practice of slavery and gave rules to make it more humane. The freeing of a slave was regarded as a meritorious act, and was prescribed as a form of expiation for certain faults.[9] The references in the Qur'ān do not give any insight into existing conditions. One word for 'slave' is *raqaba*, and there is also the expression 'what your right hands possess' (*mā malakat aymānu-kum*). What is most noteworthy is that the common word for 'slave' (*'abd*) comes to denote especially the human being in relation to God. (This is also found, of course, in the Old and New Testaments, but is disguised from English readers by being translated as 'servant' not 'slave'.)

The usual word in the Qur'ān for a kin-group is *qawm*. In English it is customary to refer to larger groups as 'tribes' and smaller groups as 'sub-tribes' or 'clans'. Later Muslim scholars gave precise definitions of half a dozen words in order of size,[10] but these are little used in early texts and not in this precise way. In practice a particular kin-group is mostly referred to as 'the sons of N' (Banū N) and it is Western scholars who decide whether it is a tribe or a clan. The only contemporary tribe mentioned by name in the Qur'ān is Quraysh (106.1), the tribe inhabiting Mecca; but it is never referred to as 'sons of', perhaps because the name was originally a nickname for a mixed group, though later they professed common descent from a man called Fihr who was nicknamed Quraysh. The word *qawm* occurs nearly four hundred times in the Qur'ān and in many cases could have the general meaning of 'people' as it is usually translated. In some of these cases, however, the probability is that to the first hearers it would suggest a kin-group, since for them this was the normal social unit. The Qur'ān usually speaks of previous prophets as having been sent each to his *qawm*.

The word *umma* occurs about fifty times in the Qur'ān, and is usually translated 'community'. It is thought to be an ancient borrowing, probably ultimately from Sumerian, and is not connected with the Arabic word for 'mother' (*umm*).[11] In the Qur'ān it is used mostly for a religious community, and doubtless was so used because people in Mecca realized that the Christians were not to be regarded as a kin-group. Much interest has been shown in the word, both in the Qur'ān and in later Islamic history,[12] but it is not important for the study of early Arabian society. Neither is the Qur'ānic word *milla*, although in its Turkish form of *millet* it became the term for a protected religious community in the Ottoman empire. In the Qur'ān *milla* means 'religion' both as a way of life and as a creed; and the phrase 'religion of Abraham' (*millat Ibrāhīm*) occurs several times.

The Qur'ān does not throw much light on the structure of the *qawm* or tribe. The most interesting point is the use of the word *mala'*. It means the leading men of a tribe collectively, and sometimes also connotes that they form a kind of council or assembly. In sūras 7, 11 and 23, where a number of earlier prophets are mentioned, it is said of each that the *mala'* of his *qawm* opposed him. Pharaoh has a *mala'* (10.75; 12.43; 26.34; etc.), and so have the Queen of Sheba and Solomon (27.29, 32, 38), and the Children of Israel (2.246; 28.20). There is also *al-mala' al-a'lā* (37.8; 38.69), which consists of all the angels or the more distinguished of them. It is a well-known fact that at Mecca there was a *mala'* which constituted a kind of senate and comprised one or two leading men from each clan; it is specifically mentioned in 38.6 as leading the opposition to belief in one God. Muḥammad's chief opponents were all members of the *mala'*. In the nomadic tribes there was probably a group which might be labelled 'leading men', but it is not clear whether they functioned as a council or were merely the main speakers in the general assembly of the tribe.

It was customary for each nomadic tribe to have a 'chief' (*sayyid*), but he was essentially *primus inter pares* and his powers were limited. The nearest to a reference to this in the Qur'ān is in 33.67 where the unbelievers say: 'we obeyed our leaders (*sādat*) and great men (*kubarā'*), and they led us astray'. Quṣayy, the effective founder of Mecca as a town, is sometimes said to have had the title of king, but what exactly this meant is not known; it may have been no more than a recognition of his personal authority. When Muḥammad was in his twenties, one of the Meccan merchants tried to get the others to recognize him as ruler of Mecca, assuring them that he could get them better terms of trade with the Byzantines; but his proposal was rejected out of hand. At Medina the man who became leader of the 'Hypocrites' had hoped, before Muḥammad's arrival, to become ruler of Medina. In both places the majority vehemently opposed having a king. The Queen of Sheba is described as telling her *mala'* that 'when kings enter a town (*qarya*) they make the great ones of its people lowly' (27.34), and this may reflect the feelings of many Arabs.

For the modern student the most important aspect of social conditions in Muḥammad's Arabia is the concept of 'protection'. This supports the solidarity of the kin-group and is supported by it. It is essentially an application of the *lex talionis* of 'life for life, eye for eye, tooth for tooth . . .'[12] It means that, where a member of one's kin-group is injured or killed, it is a sacred duty to exact the like from the offending kin-group. To modern man this may seem primitive and barbaric, but it is in fact the most effective way of maintaining a degree of public order where no single ruler or ruling group is suffiently powerful to do so; and this was, of course, the situation in Arabia. Also involved was the collective responsibility of the kin-group both for the misdemeanours of every member of the group and also for the exacting of vengeance. By the time of Muḥammad it had become common to accept blood-money (*diya*) instead of actually taking a life; the *diya* for an adult male is said to have been a hundred camels. The more puritanical among the Arabs thought that it was immoral to accept blood-money instead of an actual life, and taunted those who did so with accepting milk instead of blood.

On the whole the system worked well, though it was sometimes difficult to agree on equivalents. There was a celebrated 'war' between two tribes because one of them, after its great chief had been killed, refused to regard the life of a young man of the other tribe as adequate requital. The Qur'ān accepted the system, but tried to make it more humane by encouraging people to accept a blood-wit. It repeats the Old Testament law:

> We have prescribed for them in (the Torah):
> life for life, eye for eye, nose for nose, ear for ear,
> tooth for tooth, and for wound retaliation (*qiṣāṣ*);
> if one remits it (as alms),
> it will be an expiation (*kaffāra*) for him. (5.45)

It also prescribes retaliation for the Muslims.

> O believers, retaliation is prescribed for you for those killed,
> the free for the free, the slave for the slave,
> the female for the female, . . .
> For you in retaliation is life . . . (2.178f.)

> (The true believers are those) who when they suffer wrong
> defend themselves (*yantaṣirūn*);
> and the recompense of an evil is an evil like it . . .
> if one defends himself after being wronged,
> then against such there is no way. (42.39–41)

> If you requite, requite with the like of what you suffered;
> but if you are patient, it is better for the patient. (16.126)

It should be emphasized that the Arabs did not regard killing a person as in itself wrong. It was wrong if the person was a member of your kin-group or an allied group; and in Islam this meant the killing of any believer (4.92). Out of fear of retaliation one did not kill a member of a strong tribe. In other cases, however, there was no reason for not killing. The injunction not to kill those whose killing God has forbidden (17.33) implies that there may be some whose killing is not forbidden.

The concept of 'protection' arises out of these conditions. A person is 'protected' when there is a kin-group which is prepared to exact vengeance for him, either because he is a full member of it, or because he is attached to it. One type of attached status was that of the *jār* or 'protected neighbour' (4.36). This was probably the position of someone who was living temporarily in the area occupied by an alien tribe, but there were cases where the residence was of long duration. The term *jār* was also applied to the person granting protection; in 8.48 Satan says to those he is leading astray 'no human being will overcome you today, for I am your *jār*'; but after that he fled. To ask an individual or group for neighbourly protection is *istajāra* and to grant such protection is *ajāra* (9.6; 67.28; 72.22). The idea is applied to God in a verse which has puzzled some Western translators: 'God gives protection (*yujīru*), but no protection is given (*lā yujāru*) against him' (23.88; cf. 46.31).

Much commoner in the Qur'ān for this relation of protection is the word *walī* (pl. *awliyā'*) with its cognate *mawlā* (pl. *mawālī*). Like *jār* both can signify either the giver of protection or the one given protection; and they are often distinguished in translation as 'patron' and 'client'. In actual life one party would normally be much stronger than the other, but even in such cases some mutuality might exist, since in appropriate circumstances the weaker would give such 'help' as he could to the stronger. When groups of people are said to become *awliyā'* one of the other (for example, evildoers in 45.19), a mutual relationship is probably intended. God, as being in full control of events is frequently spoken of as *walī*.

Because of the unfamiliarity of this idea to modern Westerners, translation of the technical terms into European languages is often inadequate. The common rendering of 'friends' for *awliyā'* conceals the fact that for the first hearers it would have the connotation 'friends ready to support one by force of arms if necessary'. Another difficulty is the translation of the phrase *mā la-kum min dūn Allāh walī wa-lā naṣīr* (42.31 and many other verses). *Dūn* is an extremely elusive word which can mean either 'low and vile' or 'high and noble', and has several other meanings as well. In this phrase the common translations are 'apart from God' or 'other than God' or 'beside God'; but there are verses where such renderings are inappropriate, for example, 42.31: 'you will not frustrate (divine punishment) on earth, and you have no protector or helper *against* God'. Here and in the similar verses 11.20 and 4.123 al-Bayḍāwī makes it clear that the purpose of the *walī* and *naṣīr* is to avert the evil ordained by God. Perhaps the original idea of *min dūn* was 'to come between one and God for one's protection'. These verses raise the question whether in many more instances *min dūn Allāh* should not be translated 'against God' or something similar.

'Helper' is similarly a weak translation for *naṣīr*. The activity of the *walī* in protecting his client is described as *naṣr*, but this is not just any 'help', but help with as much force as is needed to make the 'protection' effective. It was in this sense that the Muslims of Medina were called Muḥammad's 'helpers' or Anṣār. God's support for his messengers and for the believers is *naṣr* (40.51), and the pagan deities are sometimes spoken of as if they were human rivals in the giving of *naṣr*.

> They took gods *min dūn Allāh*, hoping to be 'helped';
> but (the gods) are incapable of 'helping' them. (36.74f.)

The continuing importance of these conceptions in the expanding community of Muslims at Medina is well illustrated by 8.72.

> Those who believed and made the Hijra
> and fought with goods and person in the way of God (*sc.* the Emigrants),
> and those who gave homes and 'helped' (*sc.* the Anṣār),
> these are *awliyā'* one of the other.
> To those who believed but did not make the Hijra
> it is not for you (pl.) to give 'protection' (*walāya*)
> until they do make the Hijra.
> If they ask 'help' from you (*istanṣarū*) in respect of religion,
> it is your duty to give 'help' (*naṣr*),
> unless it is against a tribe with whom you have a treaty.

The last group are probably those who accepted Islam but continued to live with their pagan tribe, which was now making life difficult for them. This passage shows how, even when the body politic at Medina is called an *umma* with a religious basis, the details of its structure are thought of entirely in traditional Arab terms.[13]

B *'the fathers' as bearers of tradition*

The deep-rooted conservatism of the nomadic and other Arabs is closely linked with the idea of following in the steps of 'the fathers', as many passages illustrate.

> These found their fathers erring
> and themselves carried on in their steps (37.69f.)

> When it is said to them, 'Follow what God has sent down',
> they say, 'No. We follow what we found our fathers at.' (31.21)

> When it is said to them, 'Come

to what God has sent down and to the Messenger',
they say, 'Enough for us is what we found our fathers at'—
though their fathers knew nothing and were not guided.
(5.104; cf. 2.170)

Sometimes there is a trace of predestinarian views, and it is suggested that men cannot do other than follow their fathers. This can then be made into an excuse.

They said, 'Had the Merciful willed,
we would not have worshipped them (*sc.* female deities).
They have no knowledge of that but only guess.
Or did we before give them a book to which they hold fast?
Rather they say, 'We found our fathers on a way,
and in their footsteps we are guided'.
Likewise before you (Muḥammad) we sent no warner to a city
but the affluent of it said, 'We found our fathers on a way,
and in their footsteps we follow'.
He said, 'Suppose I bring you better guidance
than that of your fathers?'
They said, 'In your message we are unbelievers.'
So we punished them . . . (43.20–5)

(God said, in making a covenant with mankind as a whole:)
. . . or lest you should say, 'It was only our fathers
previously who gave partners (to you);
we were the offspring after them; will you destroy us
for what the workers of vanity did? (7.153; cf. 11.109)

When they commit an indecency (*fāḥisha*), they say,
'We found our fathers doing it, and God so commanded us'.
Say, 'God does not command indecencies'. (7.28)

Those who gave partners (to God) say, 'Had God so willed,
neither we nor our fathers
would have worshipped anything apart from him,
nor forbidden anything apart from him'.
Thus did those before them. (16.35)

In other passages it is implied that the experience of 'the fathers' is the standard by which things are to be judged. If something did not happen in the time of the fathers, it cannot happen now; if it happened then, it may also happen now.

When Moses brought them our signs as evidences,
they said, 'This is nothing but deceptive magic;
we did not hear of this among our fathers of old'. (28.36)

We sent no prophet to a town but we afflicted its people
with bad times and dearth to humble them.
Then we substituted good for evil, till they became affluent
and said, 'Our fathers experienced both dearth and wealth'
(*sc.* from natural causes, so we need not heed the messenger).
Then we afflicted them suddenly unawares. (7.94f.)

Part of the early teaching of the Qur'ān is that human beings are raised to life after death and brought to judgement. Many Meccans found this incredible, and demanded to be shown their fathers alive.

The unbelievers say, 'When we and our fathers are dust,
shall we be brought forth?
We and our fathers were promised this before;
it is only tales of the ancients.'
Say, 'Travel in the land and see
what was the end of the evildoers'.
Grieve not for them, (Muḥammad),
and be not distressed at their plotting.
(27.67–70; cf. 56.47f.; 37.16f.)

When our signs are recited to them as evidences,
their only argument is, 'Bring back our fathers,
if you speak truth'. (45.25; cf. 44.36)

This collection of quotations is sufficient to show that the conception of 'the fathers' had an important place in the thought of the pre-Islamic Arabs. The use of the plural in this connection is noteworthy. The singular 'father' occurs in the Qur'ān, but it normally refers to a single known person like the father of Joseph and his brothers. It is always 'the fathers' who are mentioned in connection with the continuity of tradition. This may be because the reference is normally to the fathers of a number of men; and it is also clear that 'fathers' may be used to include the grandfather and other male ancestors (Abraham, Ishmael and Isaac are named as the 'fathers' of Jacob—2.133; cf. 12.40). The common Arabic word for 'grandfather' does not occur in the Qur'ān. It should also be kept in mind, however, that matrilineal kinship had featured widely in Arabia at an earlier period, and was still far from extinct; and from this angle it is possible that 'fathers' was used loosely for male relatives of previous generations.

'The fathers' authoritatively exemplify the tradition of the group. In other cultures, notably peasant ones, it is usually the mothers who have this role; but the Qur'ān contains no suggestion that this was so in Arabia. The plural 'mothers' occurs ten times in the Qur'ān. In five of these it is a question of the forbidden degrees in marriage or the form of divorce known as *ẓihār* (making as the mothers' backs). One is about houses in which one may not eat, and is really akin to the point about forbidden degrees. One verse asserts that Muḥammad's wives are the mothers of the believers—which was probably tantamount to forbidding their remarriage after Muḥammad's death. The remaining three speak of children in their mothers' wombs. Thus when mothers are mentioned it is primarily in respect of physical relationships. They are not regarded as bearers of cultural tradition.

When the religion of Islam came to be proclaimed in Mecca, it was only natural that opponents should have seen it as an attack on 'the ways of the fathers', that is, traditional attitudes and beliefs. This may be illustrated by passages describing the experiences of previous prophets. Such passages, though they may have distinctive details, often reflect conditions in Mecca.

> When our signs are recited to (unbelievers) as evidences,
> they say, 'This is only a man who wants to turn you away
> from what your fathers were worshipping . . .' (34.43)

> The *mala'* of (Noah's) people, being unbelievers, said,
> 'He is only a human being like you, wanting to be above you;
> had God willed, he would have sent down an angel.
> We never heard of this among our fathers formerly.' (23.24)

> (As described by Moses, former unbelieving peoples)
> said (to their messengers), 'You are only human like us;
> you want to turn us away from what our fathers worshipped;
> so bring us clear authority.' (14.10)

> O Shu'ayb, does your prayer bid you
> that we should abandon what our fathers worshipped,
> or (cease) dealing as we please with our wealth?'
> (11.87; cf. v.62, of Ṣāliḥ)

> They said (to Moses), 'Have you come
> to turn us away from what we found our fathers at,
> so that you two may have glory in the land?
> We do not believe you two.' (10.78)

In the end the Muslims found that their religious loyalty led them not merely to break with ancestral tradition, but also to sever relationships with living kinsmen who remained pagan.

> You will not find a people believing in God and the Last Day
> who love those who oppose God and his messenger,
> even though they were their fathers, sons, brothers or clan. (58.22)

This is only 'not loving' and would not apply to Muḥammad's own clan of Hāshim under Abū-Ṭālib while they continued to support him. The next passage, however, speaks of unbelief rather than opposition and of a more complete severance.

> O believers, do not take your fathers and brothers as *awliyā'*
> if they prefer unbelief to faith;
> whoever of you is confederate with them,
> these are the wrongdoers.
> Say, 'If your fathers, sons, brothers, wives, kinsmen,
> the wealth you have acquired, the trade whose decline you fear,
> and the dwellings which please you,
> are dearer to you than God and his messenger
> and fighting in his cause,
> then wait till God brings his event;
> there is no guidance from God for the reprobate people.' (9.23f.)

The same point is made even more clearly in the story of Noah and his son.

> (The ark) was carrying them among waves like mountains;
> Noah called to his son who was apart, 'My son,
> embark with us; do not be with the unbelievers'.
> He said, 'I shall lodge in a mountain
> to save me from the water.'
> He said, 'Today there is none who saves from God's event
> except the Merciful,'
> Between the two rose the waves, and he was drowned...
> Noah called to his Lord, saying, 'My Lord,
> my son is of my family, and your promise is the truth;
> and you are the justest of judges.'
> He said, 'O Noah, he is not of your family.
> It is no upright deed.
> Ask not, where you have no knowledge.
> I exhort you not to be one of the ignorant.'
> He said, 'My Lord, I take refuge with you from asking
> where I have no knowledge; unless you forgive me
> and have mercy on me, I shall be a loser.' (11.42f., 45–7)

The words 'it is no upright deed' probably refer to the prayer Noah has made implicitly for his son, since Muslims came to regard it as sinful to pray for pagans. Abraham had done so (26.86; 19.47; 60.4), but this was permitted as the fulfilment of a promise.

> It is not for the Prophet and the believers
> to ask pardon for the pagans, even though near of kin,
> after it is clear to them that they are inmates of Hell.
> Abraham's asking pardon for his father
> was only because of a promise made to him.

When it was clear to him that he was God's enemy,
he declared himself quit of him;
Abraham was kindly and stedfast. (9.113f.)

Thus the hostility between Islam and the ancestral pagan tradition became so great that a Muslim could not even pray for a pagan father or son. Perhaps the extreme example of the severance of the ties of kinship was the son of ʿAbd-Allāh ibn-Ubayy, who offered to kill his father if Muḥammad wanted that. ʿAbd-Allāh was not strictly an unbeliever as his son asserts, but, as leader of the Hypocrites at Medina, he certainly opposed Muḥammad in political matters. Even in the story of this incident, however, as told by Ibn-Hishām, there are marks of continuing filial piety.

> ʿAbd-Allāh (the son) came to the Messenger of God and said, 'O Messenger of God, I have heard that you want ʿAbd-Allāh ibn-Ubayy killed for what has been reported to you about him. If this is so, give me the order for it and I will bring you his head. By God, the Khazraj know that they have no man more dutiful to his father than I; but I fear that, if you give the order for it to someone else and he kills him, my soul will not allow me to look at the killer of ʿAbd-Allāh ibn-Ubayy going about among the people without killing him; and thus I will kill a believer for the sake of an unbeliever, and will enter Hell.' The Messenger of God said, 'Let us be courteous with him, and behave well in his company so long as he is with us.'[14]

Despite all this hostility between fathers and sons on account of religion there remained among Muslims much reverence for the older generation.

When you have performed your rites (as pilgrims),
remember God as you remember your fathers
or more intensely. (2.200)

After the upheavals brought by the coming of Islam the fathers continued to be significant.

At this point it is worth noting that the severance of the ties of kinship is also implicit in the concept of Hijra. This is more than 'emigration' (as it is usually translated) when that is understood as a mere change of residence, because it also involved a change of *awliyā'*, that is, leaving the 'protection' of one group and entering that of another. Lane gives as a meaning for the first stem *hajara-hu* 'he cut him off from friendly or loving communion or intercourse . . . he ceased . . . to associate with him'. The third stem *hājara* (of which *muhājirūn* or 'emigrants' is the participle) has a similar meaning but connotes that the cutting is mutual. In the Qur'ān *hājara* has no object, but a phrase such as 'to God' is sometimes added.[15]

3 RELIGION IN PRE-ISLAMIC ARABIA

Much is now known about religion in pre-Islamic Arabia from a combination of archaeological and literary sources. The aim here is the limited one of presenting such information as is found in the Qur'ān. This is more than might be expected, because sometimes the words of Muḥammad's opponents are quoted before the reply is put into his mouth, and sometimes their views may be implied from the words addressed to them.

A *fatalism*

A distinctive belief of the nomadic Arab was that the main events of his life were due to the inevitable working of time. This is plainly expressed in 45.24:

> (The pagans) say, 'There is only our present life;
> we die and we live; and only Time destroys us.

By this they probably meant that sometimes a person dies and sometimes he lives, and the difference is due to Time. The word for 'Time' is *dahr*, and in the present context the translation 'fate' would not be impossible. In pre-Islamic poetry, however, misfortune, and less often good fortune, is said to be brought not only by *dahr*, but also by *az-zamān* (another word for 'time') and by 'the days' and even 'the nights'. Thus it is really the flow of temporal happenings or the course of events which the Arabs regarded as determining their lives. For them this was an impersonal force, and they do not seem to have personified Time. Neither is there any evidence of their having worshipped the Time/Fate which brought death and misfortune.[16]

Connected with the belief that Time determines the events of human life is the belief that these events are predetermined. This predetermination was accepted as a brute fact and left without explanation, while Time was seen as the efficient cause which brought the events into existence at the appropriate date. Two matters in particular were thought of as being fixed beforehand: one was the 'term' or *ajal* of a man's life, that is, the date of his death; and the other was his *rizq* or 'provision', that is, his food or sustenance. These were matters which in desert conditions it was impossible to foresee or control. Death could come from a chance encounter; and the rainfall which made the difference between abundance and starvation was completely erratic.

The Qur'ān has little to say specifically about the pagans in respect of *ajal* and *rizq*, but the two concepts are accepted into Islam and given a religious setting; and from what is then said we may form some idea of pagan views. In a sense what happened was that *dahr* was replaced by God—a point which some Muslim scholars realized and discussed.[17] The Qur'ān itself virtually asserts this, for in a verse following that in which the pagans speak of *dahr* destroying them, Muḥammad is told to reply to them:

> It is God who makes you live, then makes you die,
> then gathers you for the day of resurrection,
> about which is no doubt . . . (45.26)

Predetermined misfortune is also from God.

> No misfortune has happened
> in respect either of the land or of yourselves,
> but it was in a book before we (God) brought it about. (57.22)

The linking of predestination with a book is hardly mentioned in pre-Islamic poetry, but must have had a firm place in the thinking of the Meccans, since it appears several times in the Qur'ān. To men unwilling to take part in a campaign Muḥammad is told to say, 'Nothing will befall us except what God has written for us; he is our *mawlā*' (9.51). The *ajal* in particular is written in a book: 'no man becomes long-lived nor has any of his life cut short but it is in a book' (35.11); 'no person dies but by God's permission according to a dated book' (*kitāb mu'ajjal*) (3.145). It is worth noting that the idea is also found in the Old Testament: 'all (my actions) were recorded in your book, my days listed and determined, even before the first of them occurred'.[18]

In the Qur'ān God also becomes responsible for people's *rizq*:

> God it is who created you, then gave you provision,
> then causes you to die, then causes you to live . . . (30.40)

He is called the Provider *par excellence*, ar-Razzāq,[19] and 'the best of Providers' (*khayr ar-rāziqīn*),[20] and is usually spoken of as providing adequately. Sometimes, however, he may reduce the *rizq* either to test people or as a punishment.

> Have they not seen that for whom he wills
> God enlarges the provision or restricts it? (30.37)

The alternation of plenty and scarcity owing to the erratic character of the rainfall in the desert areas is given a theological meaning. The point was made in 7.94f. (quoted above on p.22). Dearth is sent to humble people and make them more receptive to the prophetic message, but subsequent affluence is a further test, which the pagans here fail, since they argue that dearth and wealth have always alternated through natural causes and are not determined by God as the prophet has claimed.

In an even more conspicuous fashion the pre-Islamic conception of the *ajal* or 'term' is taken over into Islam. The word has many secular usages: it can apply to a date fixed in a business contract, as for the repayment of a loan (2.282); Moses' service for his wife has an *ajal* (28.28f.), and likewise the embryo in the womb (22.5). Religiously the focus of interest is the *ajal* of each human life. This is decreed or fixed by God after each individual's creation (6.2). God also fixed an *ajal* for the heavens and the earth at their creation (30.8; 46.3), and for the sun and moon (13.2; 31.29; 35.13; 39.57). Communities as well as individuals have an *ajal* (7.34; 10.49; 15.5; 23.43); but it is implied that the 'term' of a community is the date of its punishment for unbelief. It follows from this conception that, if unbelievers are not yet punished, it is because their *ajal* has not yet been reached (cf. 16.61; etc.).

The *ajal* is always thought of as determined by God, but it has a relative fixity in that, once he has determined it, there is never any question of his altering it.

> (Noah said) Serve God and fear him, and obey me;
> he will forgive your sins, and delay you to an appointed term;
> when God's term comes it is not delayed. (71.3f.; etc.)

The fixity of the *ajal* is reinforced by the assertion sometimes made (as in 57.22 quoted above) that it is in a book. This fixity of the date of death may also be expressed without the word *ajal*. To men who thought that Muḥammad's faulty plans before the battle of Uḥud led to the loss of life there he was told to say:

> If you had been in your houses,
> those for whom being killed was written
> would have gone out to their corpse-beds. (3.154)

Another verse was probably directed to the same or similar people:

> Wherever you may be, death will seize you,
> even if you are in strong forts. (4.78)

In desert life there is much justification for a fatalistic attitude, in that it teaches one to accept with equanimity whatever happens to one. There are so many potentially destructive factors in the life of the nomad that, if he seriously tried to guard against them all, he would be so weighed down with anxiety that he would be unable to live at all in the desert. People who say, 'If our friends had stayed at home and not gone on an expedition, they would not have been killed', are described as being filled with anguish (3.156). On the other hand, fatalism may become an excuse for laziness and inactivity:

> When it is said to them,
> 'Spend of God's provision to you (to feed others)',

the unbelievers say to the believers,
'Are we to feed him whom, if God willed, he would feed?' (36.47)

As was noted above (p.21), pagans sometimes claimed that they were not responsible, since they could do no other than follow 'the fathers'.

Associated with fatalism in the outlook of the desert Arabs was what was called 'tribal humanism' in *Muḥammad at Mecca.*[21] This may be described as a belief in human excellence or manliness (*muruwwa*) as the highest value, combined with the view that the potentiality for such excellence is preserved in the tribal stock. If a man is brave and generous, it is because he is from a tribe noted for its courage and generosity. A dominant motive in most nomads was the desire to maintain the honour of the tribe. This whole outlook is abundantly illustrated in early Arabic poetry, but there is little about it in the Qur'ān except in so far as it is linked with the idea of following 'the fathers'.

B *paganism*

The Qur'ān mentions only a few of the deities known to have been worshipped in Arabia.[22] Three female deities are named in 53.19f., al-Lāt (or Allāt), al-'Uzzā and Manāt, and these had shrines in the neighbourhood of Mecca, at aṭ-Ṭā'if, Nakhla and Qudayd respectively. Five other gods are mentioned in an account of Noah (71.23): Wadd, Suwā', Yaghūth, Ya'ūq, Nasr; around 600 AD they were worshipped in Arabia, predominantly by South Arabian tribes, and seem to have been masculine. The traditional material about all these deities suggests that they had originally been agricultural or fertility powers, such as are found in the Ba'al religion of pre-Israelite Canaan. Al-Lāt is probably no more than 'the divine one' or 'the goddess' and was also known as 'the lady' (*rabba*) of aṭ-Ṭā'if; al-'Uzzā is 'the strong one'. Manāt, despite the resemblance of her name to *manāyā* ('fates'), was probably not 'a real goddess of destiny';[23] at the centre of her shrine was a rock, and this suggests an agricultural deity. The occurrence of the theophoric clan-names, Aws-Manāt and Zayd-Manāt (gift of Manāt, increase of Manāt), might even mean that to some extent she was a beneficent mother-goddess.

There is much that remains mysterious here, and the Qur'ān does not give much indication of what these deities meant to their worshippers. In so far as they were originally fertility deities, they would cease to have much meaning for those Arabs who abandoned agriculture for the life of the desert, since little of the regularity of nature was experienced there. On the other hand, many religious rites and practices were observed, especially pilgrimage. Sacred times and places also seem to have been respected for the most part. The Qur'ān has many references to pagans praying to their 'partner-gods' (*shurakā'*)—a matter to be discussed later—and there is a report of Abū Sufyān praying to the god Hubal at Uḥud.[24] Abū Sufyān is also said to have taken images of al-Lāt and al-'Uzzā with him on the expedition to Uḥud.[25] This might be what underlies the assertion in 4.76 that the unbelievers 'fight in the way of the idols' (*ṭāghūt*).

There are a number of references in the Qur'ān to the 'daughters of God' (*banāt Allāh*). All make the point that it would be ridiculous that God should have only daughters, whereas the pagans have sons.[26] What is obscure here is why the emphasis should have been on daughters when many of the idols seem to have been regarded as male. Al-Lāt and the other two female deities were certainly prominent in the mind of the Meccans as having shrines not far away; but it may also be that the Muslims felt they had a strong *argumentum ad hominem* here, since some at least of the Arabs did not like having daughters instead of sons.

> When announcement is made to one of them of a female,
> he has gloomy dark looks and is furious;
> he hides from his clan because the announcement is bad,
> (wondering) shall he keep it despite the shame
> or bury it in the dust. (16.58f.)

It is difficult to know whether there is some connection with the phrase *banāt ad-dahr* ('daughters of Time') which is found a number of times in pre-Islamic poetry.[27] The commentators on the poetry take it to mean no more than the vicissitudes of Time and the misfortunes it brings; but there are indications of a possible Iranian origin, and there it might have had an element of personification. Whether there was Iranian influence or not, the *banāt Allāh* and other deities of the Arabs were not clearly individualized or personalized, and bore no resemblance to the gods and goddesses of the Greek pantheon. Since the Arabs used words expressing kinship to denote abstract relationships, the *banāt Allāh* may be no more than 'divine beings' or 'beings with some divine qualities'.

This vagueness in the term makes it not surprising to find a number of Qur'ānic verses which suggest that the beings to whom the pagans addressed prayers were sometimes regarded as angels.[28]

> Has your Lord then distinguished you (Arabs) with sons
> and taken for himself from the angels females? (17.40)

> So ask them (Muḥammad), whether your Lord has daughters
> while they have sons;
> or did we create the angels females while they were present?
> (37.149f.)

In 34.40f. the angel-deities repudiate their worshippers.

> One day he will assemble them all,
> then say to the angels, 'Were these worshipping you?'
> They say, 'Glory to you! you are our protector against them;
> they are worshipping the jinn;
> most of them believe in them'. (34.40f.)

This apparent assimilation of deities with angels is contrary to the common view of students of Semitic religion that the worship of spirits was contrary to that of fertility powers. It may be that the assimilation was no more than a temporary expedient when the Muslims were trying to find some way of winning over their pagan opponents, especially as the deities had become somewhat detached from fertility. There is much in the Qur'ān about both angels and jinn, but apart from this identification with the goddesses they belong not to the divine world but to the created world, in which they constitute orders distinct from that of human beings. Some of the jinn even became Muslims (72.1–19).

Other points in pre-Islamic religion mentioned in the Qur'ān may be dealt with briefly. Offerings of grain and cattle (those of an agricultural people) are mentioned in 6.136 and implied in 16.56; while other verses assert that God does not require offerings of this kind constituting 'provision' (*rizq*) (20.132; 51.57). The prayer of the unbelieving Meccans at the Kaʿba is described in 8.35 as mere whistling and clapping of hands. In one verse the worship of pagan deities seems to require the sacrifice of children (6.137), but other verses speak of the killing of children for fear of want, and Muslims are forbidden to do so (17.31). Various taboos connected with 'cattle' (presumably camels) are mentioned (5,103; 6.138f.). There are also references to magic practices, notably a mysterious process of 'blowing on knots' (113.4). A defence against magic was to 'take refuge' with (*ʿādha*) some superior power. The last two sūras of the Qur'ān are formulas of 'taking refuge' against certain specified evils, and are known as the *Muʿawwidhatayn.* In these two sūras and elsewhere Muslims are encouraged to 'take refuge with God' both from Satan (7.200; 16.98; 41.36) and from men (40.56; etc.); pagans are criticized for 'taking refuge' with jinn (72.6). All this shows something of the variety of religious practice in the Arabia of 600 AD.

C *belief in* Allāh *as a 'high god'*

In recent years I have become increasingly convinced that for an adequate understanding of the career of Muḥammad and the origins of Islam great importance must be attached to the existence in Mecca of belief in *Allāh* as a 'high god'.[29] In a sense this is a form of paganism, but it is so different from paganism as commonly understood that it deserves separate treatment. Moreover there is much about it in the Qur'ān.

The first point to note is that the pagans are prepared to admit that *Allāh* is the creator of the heavens and the earth.

> If you ask them who created the heavens and the earth,
> and made the sun and moon subservient,
> they will certainly say, *Allāh* ...
> And if you ask them who sent down water from heaven
> and thereby revived the earth after its death,
> they will certainly say, *Allāh* ...
> And when they sail on the ship
> they pray to *Allāh* as sole object of devotion,
> but when he has brought them safe to land
> they 'associate' (*yushrikūn—sc.* others with him). (29.61–5)

> If you ask them who created the heavens and the earth,
> they will certainly say, *Allāh*.
> Say: Do you then consider that what you call on apart from *Allāh*,
> those (female beings) are able,
> if *Allāh* wills evil to me, to remove this evil,
> or, if he wills mercy for me, to hold back this mercy? (39.38)

In a number of other verses similar questions are asked and a similar answer given by persons who believe in other deities (31.25; 43.9–15; 87). One passage has a series of questions.

> Say: Whose is the earth and those in it ... ?
> They will say, *Allāh*'s. Say, Will you not be admonished?
> Say, Who is Lord of the seven heavens
> and Lord of the mighty throne?
> They will say, *Allāh*. Say, Will you not fear him?
> Say, In whose hand is the dominion of all things,
> (so that) he gives protection
> but no protection is given against him? ...
> They will say, *Allāh*. Say, How are you bewitched! (23.84–9)

In the immediately preceding verses it is people who disbelieve in the message with whom Muḥammad has been speaking; and the phrase 'no protection is given against him' is almost certainly to be understood of pagan deities, since in several verses (such as 39.38 above) it is stated that these deities are unable to avert God's punishment from their worshippers.

Those pagans who acknowledged *Allāh* as creator also held that the deities could intercede with *Allāh* on their behalf. This is probably the meaning of the statement that 'those who take *awliyā'* apart from

Allāh (say), We worship them only that they may bring us near to *Allāh* in intimacy' (39.3). More explicit is 10.18:

> They worship apart from *Allāh*
> what neither harms nor benefits them,
> and they say, These are our intercessors with God.

In the parable of the unbelieving town (36.13–29) the man who exhorted his fellow-citizens to follow the messengers said,

> Shall I take apart from him gods
> whose intercession, if the Merciful wills evil to me,
> will not avail me aught and will not deliver me. (36.23)

Somewhat similar is 43.86. Intercession is especially of importance on the Day of Judgement when it is said of sinners that 'among their partner-gods they have no intercessors, and they believe no more in their partner-gods' (30.12). The word rendered 'partner-gods' is *shurakā*' which means simply 'partners', but in this verse and several others it is clear from the context that they were not partners of the worshippers, but were alleged by these to be partners of *Allāh*. In one or two other verses, however (6.22,94; 10.28f.,34f.) they are spoken of as partners of the worshippers. In any case it is unlikely that the pagans themselves used the word *shurakā*'; it appears to be rather a Qur'ānic description of their attitude from the point of view of Islam.

It seems certain, however, that at least some of the Meccans regarded the deities as angels. The Qur'ān allows that angels may be intercessors.

> How many an angel is in heaven
> whose intercession is of no avail,
> save after *Allāh* gives permision
> to whoever he wills and approves. (53.26)

If asking for intercession is tantamount to worship, which implies divinity, then these angels are regarded as deities; but if this proposition is not accepted, there are two verses which speak clearly of angels being worshipped. One is 34.40f. which has already been quoted. The other is:

> The angels, who are servants of the Merciful,
> they make females . . .
> They said, Had the Merciful willed,
> we would not have worshipped them.
> They have no knowledge of that; they only guess. (43.19f.)

One verse, strangely enough, seems to involve offerings from people engaged in agriculture.

> To *Allāh* they have assigned a portion
> from the grain and the cattle he has produced,

and have said, This is for *Allāh*—as they allege—
and this for our partner-gods;
but what is for their partner-gods does not reach *Allāh*,
whereas what is for *Allāh* does reach their partner-gods. (6.136)

The interpretation of this verse is doubtful. The commentary of the Jalālayn suggests that the portion for *Allāh* went to the guests and the needy, while that for the pagan deities went to the *sadana*, the persons in charge of the shrine; but this cannot be taken as certain.

While pagans thus looked on their deities as intercessors for them with *Allāh*, it also appears that when they were in great danger they prayed to him directly. One example of this (29.65) has already been quoted. Another is 10.22:

He it is who makes you travel by land and sea;
and when you are on the ships,
and the ships run before a favouring wind
with the voyagers, and these rejoice at it,
a squally wind strikes the ships
and waves come over at the people from every quarter
and they think it is all over with them;
then they call on *Allāh* as sole object of devotion,
'If you save us from this, we shall indeed be grateful';
but when he has saved them, see,
they act unscrupulously and unjustly in the land.

Similar but less graphic is 31.32. The phrase rendered 'as sole object of devotion' is *mukhliṣīn la-hu d-dīn*, of which 'making the religion for him alone' would be a more literal translation. In these verses it seems to mean abandoning the pagan deities, at least for the time being. It would appear, then, that this phrase, which with variants occurs eleven times in the Qur'ān, is contrasting monotheism not with undifferentiated polytheism but with this belief in Allāh as a high god. The same is possibly true of the phrase *'ibādi-nā l-mukhlaṣīn*, which occurs nine times; al-Bayḍāwī (on 12.24) says that *mukhlaṣīn* means that God made them obey him alone, but notes that some scholars read the active *mukhliṣīn* throughout the Qur'ān; with either reading these 'servants' are pure monotheists. Whether *Allāh* was specially invoked in storms because he was in control of the sea is uncertain, but there is no doubt that in times of danger prayer was made to *Allāh* by believers in the pagan deities.

Some other verses may be quoted in which pagans speak of *Allāh*.

The swore by *Allāh* most solemnly,
'*Allāh* will not raise up him who dies'. (16.38)

They swore by *Allāh* most solemnly,
that if a warner came to them they would follow the guidance more than any other people;
but when a warner came to them they only rejected the more.
(35.42)

In verses already quoted pagans claim that *Allāh* commanded acts which the Qur'ān regards as indecent (7.28), and blame *Allāh* for the fact that they are pagans (16.35).

All this material goes to show that among the pagans in Mecca and presumably also in the region round there was widespread recognition of *Allāh* as high god. Such people may even have been more numerous than those who gave no special place to *Allāh*, and they may have differed among themselves about the powers of a high god. This conclusion has been reached from a study of the Qur'ān, and refers to a relatively small region during a restricted period. The study of inscriptions, however, has shown that belief in a high or supreme god was common throughout the Semitic Near East in the Greco-Roman period. It is worth quoting the conclusions of one who has made a thorough study of the inscriptions.

> The epigraphical material reveals that the worship of a supreme god coexisted with that of other minor gods. The belief that one god is able to control all the other gods, or is supreme in that he has created and looks after the world, does not constitute monotheism. But the increasing emphasis on such beliefs is evidence of a trend towards monotheism, namely towards the exclusion of other gods' existence.[30]
>
> The authors of the inscriptions worshipped a supreme god who was alone in possessing a power that excelled any other divine power. He was believed to be a Weather god; heaven belonged to him. Lesser gods were his messengers and ministers. As stated in the first chapter, the cult of the angels became a significant feature of the religious life of the Near East during the Persian and Hellenistic times. It gave the angels their role of messengers, but also stressed the fact that the Lord of Heaven ranked at the top of a hierarchy of divine beings. On the other hand, the religious life of the various groups whose inscriptions have been studied in the preceding pages was rooted in the traditions of the ancestors.[31]

In the light of this further evidence it becomes highly probable that when Muḥammad began preaching the dominant view among thinking people in Mecca was the belief in *Allāh* as high god. Pure paganism was in decline. The deities had ceased to be the natural forces familiar to an agricultural people, and seem to have had little power left except that of interceding with *Allāh*. The fact that in times of danger people turned from them to *Allāh* is a sign of their powerlessness.

D *the monotheisms*

Judaism. There are many references to the Jews in the Qur'ān, but these belong to the period after the Hijra and are mostly about the arguments they used against the Muslims and the tricks they played on them, and thus tell us virtually nothing about the Jewish communities. The material is of great importance for a study of Muḥammad's relations with the Jews, but such a study does not fall within the Meccan period. There is no record of him having any contact with Jews until he went to Medina. The verse (5.51) which tells Muslims not to take Jews and Christians as *awliyā'* since 'they are *awliyā'* one to another' probably does not mean that there is mutual support between Jews and Christians, but only that Jews support Jews and Christians support Christians.

Christianity.[32] There were one or two Byzantine Christians in Mecca, some perhaps working there temporarily as craftsmen, and Muḥammad had presumably had some contacts with Christians on his trading journeys to Syria. There was also trade between Mecca and the Christian empire of Abyssinia. This probably explains why at first the Qur'ān expressed friendship for Christians.

> You will indeed find the nearest (of the people)
> in love to the believers are those who say, We are Christians.
> That is because among them are priests and monks,
> and they are not proud. (5.82)

Another verse combines appreciation of qualities of character with a critique of monasticism.

> We gave Jesus the Gospel
> and in the hearts of his followers set kindness and mercy,
> and the monastic state; but that they invented—
> we did not prescribe it for them—
> (it was) only out of a desire to please God,
> but they did not observe it aright. (57.27)

Awareness of the divisions among Christians seems to be shown in 5.14:

> With those who say, We are Christians,
> we made a covenant;
> but they forgot a part of the admonition.
> So we stirred up enmity and hatred among them
> until the day of resurrection.

A less pleasant side of Christian life is described in 9.34, where it is not certain whether the 'scholars' are Christian bishops or Jewish rabbis, though the monks are Christian.

> O believers, many of the scholars and monks
> devour the people's wealth vainly
> and keep them from the way of God;
> they treasure gold and silver and do not spend them in the way of God.
> Give them tidings, (Muḥammad), of a painful punishment.

The Qur'ān has also many statements about Christian belief, many of them mistaken, and contrary arguments; but a detailed consideration of these does not fall within the scope of the present study.

The Ḥanīfiyya. It has often been asserted by scholars, Muslims and Westerners, that during Muḥammad's early life there was in Arabia a movement towards monotheism of which the individual participant was called a *ḥanīf*. This is based on statements by early Muslim writers, and these in turn were trying to give some background to certain Qur'ānic texts, or possibly countering the hostile suggestion that most Qur'ānic ideas came from Judaism and Christianity. In the Qur'ān itself, however, there is nothing about such a movement. All the uses of the word *ḥanīf* fall under one of the following heads.

(1) Abraham was a *ḥanīf*. This is precisely stated in 3.67: 'Abraham was not a Jew or a Christian, he was a *ḥanīf*, a *muslim*, and not one of the *mushrikīn* (idolaters).' There are similar statements about Abraham in 6.79 and 16.120.

(2) Muḥammad and the Muslims are told to follow the religion (*millat*) of Abraham as a *ḥanīf*. Thus 2.135 runs: 'They say, (We follow) the religion of Abraham as a *ḥanīf*, not one of the *mushrikīn*'. Similar, but without mention of Jews and Christian, are 3.95; 4.125; 6.161; 16.123.

(3) A similar command but without any mention of Abraham.—In 10.105 Muḥammad is told: 'Set your face to the religion as a *ḥanīf* and do not be of the *mushrikīn*'; and 30.30 is similar.

(4) The two remaining verses contain what are tantamount to commands to Muslims. The words 'be *ḥunafā*' (pl.) not *mushrikīn*' occur in 22.31 as part of instructions to be given by Abraham to would-be pilgrims to the Ka'ba. In 98.5 the People of the Book who rejected Muḥammad are told that they are commanded only 'to worship God making him sole object of devotion as *ḥunafā*'' and to perform the prayer and pay the legal alms; and prayer and alms were the basic requirement from Muslims.

There is thus not the slightest hint in the Qur'ān about a *ḥanīf* movement in the half century before Islam. The Qur'ān uses the term only of Abraham and of Muḥammad himself together with his followers and potential followers. The concept of the *ḥanīf* is in fact part of the Qur'ānic apologetic against Judaism and Christianity. The Muslims, it is claimed, are following the true religion of Abraham who was a monotheist but neither a Jew nor a Christian; and this last point is, of course, true, since Judaism took shape only some time after Abraham. It appears that for a time the religion of Muḥammad and his followers was called the Ḥanīfiyya, or the *ḥanīf*-religion. The name even occurs as a variant reading in the verse: 'the (true) religion in God's sight is the Ḥanīfiyya/Islam' (3.19).[33] How the word came to be used in the Qur'ān in this sense is not clear; in Christian Arabic and in pre-Islamic poetry *ḥanīf* means heathen or idolater.[34]

A further fact to be noted is that there is no evidence that any of the men called a *ḥanīf* by scholars ever used this name of himself or was so called by contemporaries. This means that prior to Muḥammad's mission there was no such thing as a *ḥanīf* movement so called; the movement is entirely the creation of second-century Muslim scholars such as Ibn Isḥāq, Ibn Ḥabīb and Ibn Qutayba. On the other hand, there could well have been a movement of some sort towards monotheism, fostered (as Teixidor suggests) by the belief in Allāh as high god, and the apparent powerlessness of the pagan deities. Some of the men named might have been looking for a monotheism without political implications, for Christianity was linked with the Byzantine and Abyssinian empires, and Judaism had support in the Persian empire. In effect Islam gave the Arabs a monotheism independent of the empires.

4 MECCA BEFORE ISLAM

The Qur'ān contains, at least by implication, a certain amount of information about Mecca as it was before and during Muḥammad's preaching there.

A *The sacredness of Mecca and the Ka'ba*

The territory round Mecca had for centuries been regarded as sacred, and special sanctity was attached to the Ḥaram or 'sanctuary area' immediately round the Ka'ba. It was probably the Ka'ba, and in particular the Black Stone set into it, which was the basis of the sacred character of Mecca. The Qur'ān accepts the pre-Islamic belief in the sacredness of the Ka'ba and of the whole region, but sees this as coming from God. Muḥammad is told to say:

> I am commanded only to serve the Lord of this place (*balda*),
> who made it sacred, and to whom everything belongs. (27.91)

Another verse referring to unbelievers runs:

> Have they not seen that we have appointed a sanctuary (*ḥaram*) secure,
> while around them the people are plundered? (29.67)

Meccan affairs are the subject of Sūra 106.

> For the *īlāf* of Quraysh,
> the *īlāf* of the caravan of the winter and the summer,
> let them worship the Lord of this House,
> who against hunger has fed them,
> and against fear has given them security.

The use of the phrase 'the Lord of this House' makes it likely that those Meccans who believed in *Allāh* as a high god—and they may have been numerous—regarded the Ka'ba as his shrine, even though there were images of other gods in it. There are stories in the Sīra of pagan Meccans praying to *Allāh* while standing beside the image of Hubal.[35] The word *Ilāf* is vocalized and interpreted in various ways, such as 'assembling' or 'bringing together'. Whatever the exact interpretation, the first two verses refer to the commercial activities of the Meccans, while the last two describe aspects of their commercial prosperity. They are able to import sufficient food to keep themselves well supplied, and they are threatened by no enemies. The 'security' may be due in part to the sacredness of the Meccan territory, but the wealth of Mecca and its economic power must also have contributed to their feeling of being safe. In so far as the expedition with the elephant described in Sūra 105 was directed against Mecca and was foiled by God, this would be another example of his giving the Meccans security (p.15 above).

B *Mecca as a commercial centre*

The commercial character of Mecca is evident in many ways from the Qur'ān. The absence of agriculture is indicated in a speech by Abraham:

> I have caused some of my descendants
> to dwell in a valley without cultivated land
> at your sacred house. (14.37)

Among the matters for which Quraysh are to thank God are their winter and summer caravans (106.2); traditionally the caravans went to the Yemen in winter and to Syria in summer. The Sīra shows that there were also close relations between Mecca and the Abyssinian kingdom; and the numerous references in the Qur'ān to ships and the sea suggest that many Meccans may themselves have made the journey to Abyssinia.[36] In the parable of the blighted garden in 68.17–33 (p.12 above), though this is an agricultural rather than a commercial matter, the unfeeling self-seeking of the owners could indicate the operations of a Meccan syndicate.

The development of Mecca as a commercial centre was partly due to its geographical position about the middle of the caravan route up the west coast of Arabia from the Yemen, and at the beginning of a route to Iraq. It was also facilitated by the existence of the sanctuary, since in the sacred territory blood feuds were in abeyance and there was therefore some security for men to come together at trade fairs. Certain months were also regarded as sacred, and it was during these that the fairs took place. One verse indicates the dependence of Meccan prosperity on the sanctuary:

> Have we not established for them a sanctuary secure
> to which the fruits of everything are brought,
> as a provision from us? (28.57)[37]

This presumably refers to the collecting of goods for trade purposes, since it must be supposed that local produce, whether from the herds or from the land, was brought to Mecca to be exchanged for the goods carried by caravan from Syria, the Yemen and Iraq. The people to whom these words are addressed are said to be afraid that, if they 'follow the guidance', they may forcibly be removed from their land. This is obscure; the most likely meaning is that they were afraid that, if they followed Muḥammad, the surrounding Arabs would cease to observe the sanctity of Mecca and would raid the town-dwellers. In a verse (9.28) debarring pagans from the Kaʿba, revealed after the capture of Mecca in 630, the words 'if you fear poverty . . .' are a further indication of the wealth derived from those who came to the sanctuary for trade and worship.

The American scholar C. C. Torrey made a careful study of all the commercial metaphors used in the Qur'ān, and came to the conclusion that in some cases they were not used incidentally or by way of illustration, but expressed some of the central theological teaching of the Qur'ān.[38] This is precisely what we should expect in a commercial centre. The points made by Torrey have been well summarized.

> The number of commercial terms transferred to the religious sphere is noteworthy . . . The deeds of men are recorded in a book; the Judgement is the reckoning; each person receives his account; the balance is set up and men's deeds are weighed; each soul is held in pledge for the deeds committed; if a man's actions are approved, he receives his reward, or his hire; to support the Prophet's cause is to lend to (God).[39]

There are even indications in the Qur'ān that in the years of Muḥammad's success some of the Muslims continued to be so addicted to trade that they showed much more interest in that than in worship:

> In (these houses) there give praise to God morning and evening
> men whom neither merchandise nor bargain lure
> from remembrance of God,
> from the offering of prayer and the giving of alms. (24.36f.)

> When they see merchandise or play, they disperse to it
> and leave you standing. Say: What is with God is better
> than play and merchandise; and God is the best of providers.
> (61.11)

C *attitudes to wealth*

The numerous passages in the Qur'ān describing and criticizing wealthy people for their attitudes and their acts may be taken as applying primarily to the great merchants of Mecca. It has also to be remembered, of course, that in the background of their lives was the life of the desert, and that at some points they were reacting to that.

A primitive stage in Arab experience is reflected in the verb *ghaniya* and its derivatives. The adjective *ghanī* is commonly translated 'rich' or 'wealthy', but the fundamental meaning of the verb is 'to be free from want, to have few or no wants'. From this meaning others are derived such a 'to be in a state of sufficiency, to be rich'. In the life of the desert what is important is to have sufficient to eat and drink. The nomad must, of course, have a tent and other simple equipment, but more than a limited number of material possessions would be an encumbrance rather than an advantage. It is noteworthy that in most of the instances of *ghanī* in the Qur'ān it is applied to God, since only to him can the complete absence or non-existence of wants be attributed. It is interesting, too, that *ghaniya* has the sense of 'dwell, lodge' in the phrase 'as if they had not dwelt (*lam yaghnaw*) there', which is used twice of Midian (7.92; 11.95) and once of Thamūd (11.68). The underlying thought is perhaps that the nomad, so long as he has a sufficiency, continues to lodge in the same place.

The new aspects of experience which came to the Arabs after they settled in towns and engaged in trade are indicated in the Qur'ān in verses containing the word *māl*, plural *amwāl*, 'wealth, property, possessions'. In 48.11 when the nomads excuse themselves for their absence from the expedition to al-Hudaybiya by saying their *amwāl* and their families kept them busy, by *amwāl* they presumably mean their herds of camels and other animals. Mostly in the Qur'ān, however, *māl* and *amwāl* refer to the material goods bought, sold and stored up by the merchants. 'Sons' or 'children' are frequently mentioned along with 'wealth', doubtless because both were a reason for pride and also a source of influence in the community; in 34.35 affluent unbelievers in a prophet say, 'We have more wealth and sons, and we shall not be punished'.

Various attitudes accompanied the possession of wealth. Thus in 104.1–3 the Meccan opponents who kept slandering Muḥammad and the Muslims are described as not merely amassing wealth but as thinking that it will make them immortal. The same people are accused in 102.1 of being occupied with *at-takāthur*, wanting to have more than others, presumably in respect of wealth and children. These last are specifically mentioned in 57.20:

> Know that this present life is play and outward show;
> it is emulous boasting with one another
> and *takāthur* in respect of wealth and children.

Rejection of a prophet's message seems to be frequent among the wealthy, as was certainly the case in Mecca.

> We never sent a warner to a town
> but the affluent in it said, 'In your message we disbelieve'.
> They also said, 'We are superior in wealth and children,
> and we are not punished'.

The implication appears to be that because they were wealthy they would not suffer the disasters foretold by the prophets. Elsewhere, how ever, it is pointed out that the wealthy are not immune from disaster.

> (The hypocrites and unbelievers will be punished) like those before you;
> these were greater in strength than you
> and superior in wealth and children . . .
> the acts of these men are worthless in this world and the next,
> and they are the losers. (9.69)

For these affluent people a man's wealth was a criterion of his position in society and his personal authority. The Meccans would have approved of the attitude of the children of Israel when they objected to the appointment of Ṭālūt (Saul) as king over them, saying 'he has not been given abundance of wealth' (2.247). Since the wealthy thus regard wealth as the criterion of a man's worth and importance, it is not surprising that they manifest attitudes of arrogance and presumption. Such attitudes are connected with their rejection of the messages from God.

> Presumptuous indeed is man,
> thinking himself (by his wealth) independent (*istaghnā*);
> but to your Lord is the return (to be judged). (96.6–8)

Similarly the man 'who is ungenerous and wealth-proud (*istaghnā*) and denies the fairest (message)' will have his way to punishment made easy, and 'his wealth will not avail him when he perishes' (92.8–11). In Sūra 80 Muḥammad himself is reproached for observing Meccan standards and being unduly attentive to a man who was 'wealth-proud'. The word *istaghnā* used here combines the ideas of priding oneself in one's wealth and feeling independent; it is a derivative of *ghaniya.*

The idea that a wealthy man who disregards what he has been told about God, even by a friend, will be punished is expressed fully in the story of the man with two gardens (18.32–44; mentioned on p.11 above). The main point here is that the wealthy man, though nominally believing in God and the Judgement, does not take these beliefs seriously and does not act upon them. Opponents of Muḥammad at Mecca and even at Medina seem to have assumed that, even if there is a Judgement, they will receive preferential treatment at it in the way in which the wealthy could count on being given special consideration in human judgements; hence the warnings in the Qur'ān that wealth will not avail or profit a man at his death or at the Judgement. In a description of the Last Day one of the damned says, 'My wealth has not profited me' (69.28); and Abraham in a prayer speaks of 'the day when wealth and sons give no advantage' (26.88). The implication is that it is against God that wealth is of no avail and does not profit, and this is sometimes explicitly stated, as in 3.10, 116; 58.17.

Acceptance of the message revealed through Muḥammad or one of the previous prophets leads to a change in a man's use of his wealth. The people of Shu'ayb are perturbed because they are required not merely to give up their fathers' idols but also to give up doing what they want with their wealth (11.87). What the Muslims are commanded to do or are described as doing is presumably what the wealthy in Mecca were not doing. The pious Muslim does not hoard his wealth and is not ungenerous with it (92.18; 9.103); he gives a proportion of it to the poor and unfortunate (51.19; 70.24); and he is honest in administering the property of orphans (4.2,5,10; 6,152; 17.34). Many of Muḥammad's followers in Mecca shared in the general attitude to wealth and found it difficult, on becoming Muslims, to abandon it. In 2.177 (according to the most likely translation) the ideal life is said to consist, among other things, in a man's giving of his wealth *despite his love of it* to those in need; and the believers are warned that wealth and children are a 'trial' (*fitna*) for them (8.28; 64.15), and that they must not allow these to distract them from the remembrance of God (63.9).

There is little in the Qur'ān about the virtue of *ḥilm* for which the wealthy men of Mecca were renowned. *Ḥilm* is essentially the opposite of the hotheadedness of the desert Arabs who rush into violent action when the blood is up; and thus it comes to mean the coolheadedness of the business man who puts business interests first. The common translation 'forbearance' is not altogether adequate. There may be a reference to this quality in 52.32 where the plural occurs: 'Do their *aḥlām* bid them act thus (*sc.* deny the truth of Muḥammad's proclamation)?' The word *aḥlām* could appropriately be understood of the minds of business men calculating in an unemotional way. To those utterly convinced of the truth of the Qur'ān it must have seemed that the Meccans, in opposing Muḥammad, were not even following the course indicated by enlightened self-interest and were not displaying their usual coolheadedness. Their self-centred attitude is clearly expressed in 70.11–14 which depicts the feelings of unbelievers on the Last Day:

> The sinner would love to be ransomed from the punishment of that Day
> by his sons, his wife, his brother,
> by his kin who shelter him
> and those in the earth altogether . . .

This illustrates the breakdown of social solidarity and its replacement by individualism and selfishness, largely as a result of the predominantly mercantile economy of Mecca.

D *knowledge of Judaism and Christianity*

It is important to have some idea of what the Meccans in general knew about Judaism and Christianity. Some of the statements about these religions in the Qur'ān are palpably false, and it was suggested above that this was because these were beliefs held by the Meccans and that God addressed them in terms of their existing beliefs, since the Qur'ānic message could be communicated to them without correcting these beliefs.

The Meccans had numerous contacts with Christians. Their trading caravans took them to the Christian cities of Damascus and Gaza in the Byzantine empire, as well as to Christian Abyssinia and the partly-Christian Yemen. A few Christians also resided in Mecca itself, at least temporarily. There were hardly any Jews in Mecca, but the Jews were numerous in Medina, where Meccan caravans to the north sometimes made a stop. Such contacts could, of course, lead to no more than an external knowledge of these religions, and it is probable that few Meccans engaged in religious discussions. We are told in the Sīra, however, of one or two who had read some of the Christian scriptures (presumably in Syriac) and who eventually became Christians. The best known of these was Waraqa, Khadīja's cousin. This knowledge of the Bible is presumably what the Qur'ān refers to in the words 'your Lord . . . taught by the pen, taught people what they knew not' (96.3–5).

The presence in Mecca of one or more persons with some knowledge of the Bible would seem to be attested by two verses which record Meccan accusations that Muḥammad had informants.

> We know they say, It is only a person teaches him.
> The tongue of the one they hint at is foreign,
> but this (the Qur'ān) is (in) a clear Arabic tongue. (16.103)

> The unbelievers say, This is only a falsehood he invented;
> other people helped him with it . . .
> They said, Old-world fables, he has had written down;
> they are dictated to him morning and evening. (25.4f.)

There is no agreement among the Muslim commentators about the identity of the person 'hinted at'. Several names are given, mostly of Christian slaves in Mecca, but of at least one Jew. As is suggested in the second verse quoted, there may well have been more than one person. What is important to notice is that the Qur'ān does not deny that Muḥammad was receiving information in this way; what it insists on is that any material he received could not have been the Qur'ān, since a foreigner could not express himself in clear Arabic. The probability would seem to be that Muḥammad talked about Biblical matters with people who knew more than the average inhabitant of Mecca, but what he received from them must have been limited in scope in view of the paucity of his knowledge of Judaism and Christianity. What he was given would be factual knowledge, whereas the meaning and interpretation of the facts would come to him by the usual processes of revelation.

The references in the Qur'ān to the Old Testament prophets and patriarchs are cast in a form which suggests that at least some of the hearers already had an idea of the outline of the stories, and that what the Qur'ān was doing was to point the lessons to be learnt from these stories; for example, they show how God defends his prophets from their opponents. The chief error in the Qur'ān in respect of Judaism is the assertion that the Jews regarded Ezra ('Uzayr) as 'son of God' (9.30); while it is true that the Old Testament uses the term 'son of God' for the Messiah who was expected, there is no evidence that it was ever applied to Ezra.

The Qur'ān shows that there was little knowledge in Mecca of the New Testament apart from the story of the virginal conception of Jesus (19.16–21). On the other hand several mistaken ideas about Christianity appear to have been current among the Meccans. They supposed that Christians worshipped three gods, taking both Jesus and Mary as gods.

Most serious of all they denied that Jesus had died on the cross (4.157). There was no appreciation or understanding of the central teachings of the New Testament.

III

Muḥammad's Early Life

I FAMILY AND MARRIAGE

It is only to be expected that the Qur'ān tells us little about the circumstances of Muḥammad's life before his call to be a messenger of God. Apart from Sūra 93 (to be considered presently) all that can be gained are some confirmations of the general conditions in which he lived from infancy to early manhood.

There was doubtless a strong bond of attachment between him and his mother, with whose family he is said to have lived until her death when he was six. The following verse, though Medinan, may be in keeping with what his own attitude was:

> We have enjoined man in regard to his parents—
> his mother bore him in great weakness, and his weaning was at two years—
> 'Show gratitude to me and to your parents'. (31.14)

Another similar verse runs:

> We have enjoined kindness on man in regard to his parents;
> in pain his mother carried him and in pain brought him forth;
> his carrying and his weaning are thirty months.
> Then when he reaches maturity, reaches forty years,
> he says, My Lord make me grateful
> for the favour you have shown me and my parents ... (46.15)

Though 2.233 says that suckling is normally to be for two years, the Sīra suggests that Muḥammad may have been suckled for longer, since he was sent for a time to a wet-nurse in a nomadic tribe. The Qur'ān bears witness to the practice of giving children to foster-mothers. A part of the verse mentioned (2.233) asserts that 'if you want to give your children out to nurse, it is no sin for you' (*lā junāḥ ʿalay-kum*); and this suggests that the practice may have been criticized in some quarters and that Muḥammad may have been sensitive about it. Another verse (65.6), after emphasizing that a man must maintain his wife adequately while she is suckling his child, adds that, 'if there are difficulties between you, let another (woman) be found to give suck for (the husband)'. The fact that Muḥammad was a posthumous child may, of course, have been part of the reason for sending him to a wet-nurse.

As a small boy Muḥammad must soon have realized that he was different from other boys in having no father alive. He may have been bitter about his position, perhaps even—to judge from modern instances—may have felt resentment against the father who had abandoned him. His grandfather ʿAbd-al-Muṭṭalib doubtless acted as a father towards him in some respects, especially after his mother's death. There are stories in the Sīra which imply a close relation between the two; but ʿAbd-al-Muṭṭalib died when Muḥammad was eight, and thus he was again abandoned. The next father-figure was Abū-Ṭālib, who succeeded his father as chief of the clan of Hāshim, and who is said to have taken his nephew Muḥammad with him to Syria on trading journeys. Although he did not approve of Muḥammad's teaching, he supported him, as honour required, against those who were hostile to it. The following verse is primarily addressed to followers whose parents were trying to stop them being Muslims, but it may reflect something of Muḥammad's own attitude:

> If they two try to prevail on you to associate with me (God)
> what you have no knowledge of, do not obey them;
> but dutifully bear them company in this world
> and follow the way of one who turned wholly to me.
>
> (31.15; cf. 29.8)

It has already been noted (p.21) that pagans make 'following the fathers' an excuse for not becoming Muslims. Something of Muḥammad's own unconscious bitterness at the father-figures who abandoned him may find expression in the attacks of the Qur'ān on the fathers as bearers of ancestral tradition and opponents of religious truth.

There is no definite evidence in the Qur'ān for any journeys made by Muḥammad. That Meccan merchants made journeys is confirmed by the reference to the winter and summer caravans in 106.2. Despite the story in the Sīra of Muḥammad's meeting with the monk Baḥīrā, there is nothing in the Qur'ān to show that he had any contact with Christians. On the contrary it has been argued that, if the passage about the table to be sent down from heaven (5.112-5) is to be regarded as an account of the Christian eucharist, then it shows that Muḥammad had never personally observed the Christian liturgy.[1] In the passage describing a storm at sea (10.22; quoted on p.34) some would hold that the vividness of the description implied personal experience of a storm; and in that case Muḥammad must have voyaged across the Red Sea to Ethiopia. On the other hand, descriptions of such experiences may have been familar to many in Mecca.

The most important reference to Muḥammad's early life is in Sūra 93, which may be quoted in full:

> Your Lord has not abandoned you nor hated you,
> but the last will be better for you than the first,

and in the end your Lord will give to your satisfaction.
Did he not find you an orphan and house you?
find your erring and guide you?
find you poor and enrich you?
So oppress not the orphan,
repulse not the beggar,
but declare the favour of your Lord.

The word 'orphan' accords with the traditional account that Muḥammad was a posthumous child and that his mother died when he was young. Orphans, as long as they were minors, had few rights in Arabian society, and so their need was for 'protection' (in the technical sense) as well as for the material necessities of food and shelter. This is implied by the words 'oppress not the orphan'. The word *awā*, translated 'house you', has also the connotation of protecting from oppression; and this was indeed done for Muḥammad by his grandfather and by his uncle Abū-Ṭālib.

Some problems are raised by the word 'erring' (*ḍāll*). It has been maintained both in Islam and in other religions that a religious leader must be perfect in his religion even before the period of his leadership. This seems to go back to an infantile demand for perfection or inerrancy in the parents, and unwillingness to admit the extent of imperfection and weakness in the grown-up world. It follows that, where inerrancy is ascribed to a religious leader, it is a projection on to him by his followers and not a matter of observation; for this reason it will normally be discounted. From a modern standpoint it does not seem to impair Muḥammad's prophethood to admit that for the first forty years of his life he had accepted the views commonly held by the upper strata of Meccan society. To judge from the witness of the Qur'ān to pre-Islamic religion and from the story of the 'satanic verses', Muḥammad's original belief may have been in *Allāh* as 'high god' or supreme deity, combined with lesser local deities whom he may have come to regard as angels who could intercede with the supreme being. There is even a report that he said that he had once sacrificed a sheep to al-ʿUzzā.[2] Whatever the precise views he held— and they may have changed as he grew older— the word 'erring' would be a description of his outlook before he received 'guidance'. In 62.2, when a messenger is sent to the 'gentiles' (*ummiyyīn*), he recites God's signs to them, appoints Zakāt for them, and teaches them the Book and wisdom; and as a result they cease to be in a state of *ḍalāl* or error. The guidance received by Muḥammad would therefore appear to be what came to him by revelation.

This conclusion receives some confirmation from 4.113:

> God sent down upon you (Muḥammad) the Book and the wisdom,
> and taught you what was unknown to you.

These words occur in a passage probably not revealed until after the battle of Uḥud, charging 'a party of them' with desiring to lead Muḥammad astray. The most likely reference would be to some event at Medina, but it is conceivable that it might refer to attempts of the Meccans before the Hijra to 'lead him astray' by engulfing him in commerce. In either case it is implied that there was a period when Muḥammad did not know some of what came to him by revelation. His original ignorance is also mentioned in 42.52:

> We revealed to you a spirit from our *amr* (sphere?);
> unknown to you what the Book was, what faith was,
> but we made it (spirit?, Book?) a light
> by which we guide whom we will of our servants.

Finally there is the verse in Sūra 93 about being poor and then enriched. The obvious reference is to Muḥammad's marriage to Khadīja, and it is unlikely that he could have been enriched at any other point before the Hijra (and the passage is always taken as Meccan). By Arab laws of inheritance, where minors do not inherit and there is no representation (in the legal sense), Muḥammad would inherit neither from his father nor his grandfather. The fortunes of the family, too, seem to have been declining. Thus he remained poor until Khadīja made him her steward and subsequently married him, when he was about twenty-five. Afterwards he would be comfortably off, though not one of the leading merchants; this is implied in 43.31 where opponents say, 'Why was not this Qur'ān sent down to some important man (*'aẓīm*) of the two towns (Mecca and aṭ-Ṭā'if)?'. The word *aghnā*, 'enriched', besides referring to the possession of money or goods, connotes having a place of relative independence and influence in the community.

Traditionally there were about fifteen years between this marriage and the beginning of the revelations. It was probably his exclusion from the most lucrative trade, coupled with his consciousness of having great organizing ability, that made Muḥammad turn to brood over the general state of affairs in Mecca. Despite his financial dependence on Khadīja he was definitely head of the household. Such at least is the natural deduction from 20.132: 'Command your *ahl* to pray'. The word *ahl* is often translated 'family', but it can also mean 'wife' and should probably be so translated here; even if it means 'family' the primary reference is to the wife.

Insight is given by the last three verses of the sūra into Muḥammad's attitude to his early life. Psychology teaches us the importance of painful experiences in the first two or three years of life. The absence of a father must have produced a sense of deprivation in Muḥammad, and the real experience of poverty as a young man may well have nourished the sense of deprivation. These verses assert that, despite the unfortunate circumstances of his early life, God's care and activity on Muḥammad's behalf have made life tolerable; and then he is commanded to try to meet the needs of those in similar troubles and to speak of God's favour. In this the Qur'ān is presumably only reinforcing an attitude Muḥammad had already adopted, rather than suggesting something novel. Even if there is an element of novelty in these verses, however, the implication is that Muḥammad eventually came to see his orphanhood, poverty and lack of guidance as aspects of the ordering of his life by God the Merciful, and perhaps also as a preparation for his work as Messenger of God. After this revelation, as he looked back on his early life, he must have been most conscious of the favour or goodness of God.

During the years just before he received the call to prophethood Muḥammad must have been increasingly aware of the unsatisfactory social conditions in Mecca. This was something he could observe for himself and did not require to be shown by revelation. The fundamental source of the trouble was that the traditional values of nomadic society (which was that of the recent ancestors of the Meccans) were proving inadequate in the prosperous mercantile economy of Mecca, and were fading away. The wealthy merchants, who were also the leading men of the clans, were neglecting the traditional duty of caring for the needy and unfortunate among their kinsmen. Their great wealth made them proud, arrogant and presumptuous, ready to oppress and take advantage of any who were in any sense weak. Some of the Qur'ānic evidence for these attitudes was presented in the last chapter. Muḥammad may well have come to see the root of the troubles as the secular, materialistic outlook of the very wealthy, and may even have decided that this could only be got rid of by some form of religious belief. It is impossible, however, to know what precisely his religious views were prior to the divine irruption into his life which was inspiration and revelation.

2 THE QUESTION OF LITERACY

There has been much discussion about whether Muḥammad could read or write. The main body of later Muslim opinion argued that the revelation of the Qur'ān was all the greater miracle because Muḥammad could neither read nor write; and the weight of this argument rests on the dubious interpretation of the word *ummī* as 'illiterate', which will be looked at presently. Various other points, however, can be made from the Qur'ān.

The Meccans were in general familar with reading and writing. A certain amount of writing would be necessary for commercial purposes. The Sīra speaks of the treaty of al-Hudaybiya having been written, and texts have been preserved of other treaties entered into by Muḥammad. Muḥammad is also reported to have sent letters to various princes, and for these he presumably had scribes. In the Qur'ān there are references to the words of God being written with pens and ink (31.27; 18.109). Scriptures are written on *qirṭās,* probably papyrus (6.7, 91), or on *raqq,* probably parchment (52.3). The material was in the form of *ṣuḥuf* or 'leaves' (sing. *ṣaḥīfa*), but these could also be used for keeping records (8.10; perhaps also 74.52), and so may also have been used for commercial records; the word probably comes from South Arabian.[3] Another word for 'writings' is *zubur*; in 54.52 all men's deeds are inscribed on *zubur.* The singular *zabūr,* however, is used in the Qur'ān exclusively for the Psalms of David. In 21.104 God is said to roll up the heavens as a written scroll (*sijill*) is rolled up. Even at Medina (2.28f) there were numerous scribes who could write down debts.

In view of this familiarity with writing among the Meccans particularly, both for records and for religious scriptures, there is a presumption that Muḥammad knew at least enough to keep commercial records. There are, on the other hand, many reasons for thinking that he had never read the Bible or any other book. For one thing, if a copy of the Bible existed in Mecca, it must almost certainly have been in a Syriac version. Though some Western scholars have held that the Bible had been translated into Arabic, this was virtually impossible, since at this period there was no Arabic prose literature of any kind. If a man like Waraqa or some of Muḥammad's alleged informants had read any of the scriptures, it was presumably in Syriac. Such scriptures were almost certainly intended by the assertion that God 'taught by the pen, taught people what they knew not' (96.4f). That Muḥammad himself had not read any scriptures is clearly stated in 29.48; 'you were not reciting/reading any book before it (the Qur'ān), nor tracing it with your hand'. The accusation of pagan opponents that his revelations were 'old-world fables *iktataba-hā*' (25.5) can mean 'he had them written down for him (by secretaries)' and so does not necessarily imply that he himself wrote them down. The probability is that Muḥammad was able to read and write sufficiently for business purposes, but it seems certain that he had not read any scriptures.

This conclusion gives Muslim scholars all that is essential for apologetic purposes. They have, however, argued that the word *ummī* which is applied to Muḥammad implies complete inability to read and write. One of their arguments is that the plural *ummiyyūn* in 2.78 means 'illiterate' or 'unlettered': 'among them are *ummiyyūn* who do not know the book except from hearsay'. The rendering 'except from hearsay' (which is Pickthall's) is much disputed but hardly affects the argument. While *kitāb* suggests writing as well as 'book', careful reading of the verse shows that the reference is to people without a written scripture, and Pickthall in fact translates *kitāb* as 'scripture'. This meaning suits the other instances where the plural occurs. In 3.75 some of the People of the Book say, 'We are not bound to justice in respect of the *ummiyyūn*'; and from this it may be concluded that the word has been adopted from the People of the Book, that is, the Jews. The Jews, however, applied it to others and not to themselves, for in 3.20 Muḥammad is commanded, 'Say to the People of the Book and the *ummiyyūn*, Have you surrendered (to God)?' The *ummiyyūn*, then, must be the non-Jews or Gentiles, who had no written scriptures and were in fact 'heathen' (as often translated); the word has presumably been derived from the Hebrew phrase *ummōt hā-'ōlām*, 'the peoples of the world' or *gentes*.

This sense of *ummī* as 'Gentile' or 'unscriptured' fits the verses where it is applied to Muḥammad.

> (God) it is who sent among the *ummiyyūn* a messenger,
> (one) of themselves, to recite to them his signs,
> to purify them, and to teach them the Book and the wisdom,
> though before they were in clear error. (62.2)

Again God is described as saying to Moses that his mercy will be 'written' for those 'who follow the messenger, the *ummī* prophet, whom they find written in the Torah and the Evangel which they have ...' (7.157). In the next verse Muḥammad is commanded to address all the people and to conclude with the words: 'so believe in God, his messenger, the *ummī* prophet, who believes in God and his words' (7.158). Thus the *ummī* prophet is the non-Jewish or Gentile prophet, whom Muslims held to be foretold in the Bible, and who was sent by God to his own non-Jewish or heathen people, as well as to the Jews and perhaps the Christians. Thus *ummī* does not mean 'illiterate' in the strict sense, though it could be rendered 'unscriptured'; but this still means—as is indeed obvious—that Muḥammad had no direct knowledge of the Bible.[4]

IV

Muḥammad's Prophetic Experience

The aim of this chapter is to discover what can be learnt from the Qur'ān about Muḥammad's call to be a prophet and his subsequent experiences of prophethood. There is much about these matters in the Sīra-material, but it is less reliable, and the accounts of the call in particular have little of genuine historical value. While the commonest title for Muḥammad in Arabic is 'Messenger of God' (*rasūl Allāh*), the associations of the English word 'messenger' are mainly secular, and it is thus better to take 'prophet' as the normal term in English, especially as it has derivatives such as 'prophetic' and 'prophethood'.

1 THE FIRST THREE YEARS

The view most commonly held is that the call to be a prophet came to Muḥammad thirteen years before the Hijra, that he then began to receive revelations (those which now constitute the Qur'ān), and that for three years he communicated them only to friends. Then ten years before the Hijra he began to proclaim his message publicly.[1] Unfortunately there are several alternative versions of these events.[2] The main conclusion to be drawn from all this material would appear to be that there were two climactic points in Muḥammad's experience of prophethood, one thirteen years before the Hijra and the other ten. The problem then becomes to discover if there are any differences between the first three years and the period after the second point.

Traditionally, Muḥammad was about forty when he was given the prophetic vocation, and this is roughly confirmed by the Qur'ān. It is implied in 10.16 that Muḥammad was a mature man before the revelation came to him and had remained a lifetime (*ʿumur*) among the Meccans; and while *ʿumur* cannot be given a precise meaning, it is to be noted that in 46.15 maturity is identified with the age of forty years. The conventional date for the first coming of revelation is the year 610, and this may be taken as the first climactic point, so that the second would be in 613. By inclusive reckoning these are thirteen and ten years respectively before the Hijra in 622.

The usual account of the call to prophethood is that Gabriel appeared to Muḥammad and told him, 'You are the Messenger of God'. He also commanded him to recite, and expanded this command into the first verses of Sūra 96:

> Recite in the name of your Lord who created,
> created man from a blood-clot;

recite, for your Lord is most generous,
who taught by the pen,
taught people what they knew not. (96.1-5)

Such in this account was the beginning of revelation. The many variants may be disregarded here; in particular the versions which require the command *iqra'* to be understood as 'read' (a possible meaning) instead of 'recite' must belong to later Muslim apologetic.

To the modern scholar it is virtually certain that what happened was different from what is asserted here. For one thing it is only after the Hijra that Gabriel appears in the Qur'ān as the bearer of revelation (2.97). There is even an explicit statement in the Sīra that during the first three years the angel who came to Muḥammad was Isrāfīl. Again it seems impossible that the term *rasūl Allāh* could have had any clear meaning for Muḥammad at this date; as will be seen in section 4 it was only gradually that the full implications of Muḥammad's prophetic vocation became clear. With regard to the first revelation there is an alternative account which claims it was Sūra 74, 'O thou enwrapped, rise and warn . . .' Both of these accounts may be no more than the guesses of later scholars. It is appropriate that a book called the Qur'ān or Recitation should begin with the word 'Recite'; the words 'Rise and warn' are also appropriate for the beginning of a prophetic mission. Western scholars like Sir William Muir and Hubert Grimme held that several short sūras had been revealed before 96 and 74. This is not impossible, but there can be no certainty about it. The safest conclusion is that we do not know how the verbal revelations began which now constitute the Qur'ān. It seems unlikely that either 96 or 74 marked the first climactic point, though 74 might have marked the second, and the word 'Warn' in it may indicate the beginning of public proclamation. This would make it likely that, for at least the greater part of the three-year period, Muḥammad was not receiving verbal revelations, though the mention of Isrāfīl suggests that he may have been receiving some other form of inspiration. It is also likely that, even if the precise form of words 'You are the Messenger of God' has to be rejected, Muḥammad somehow or other became convinced that he had a special vocation. This would then be the first climactic point thirteen years before the Hijra. In the Sīra-material there is a statement attributed to 'Ā'isha to the effect that what was the very beginning of Muḥammad's prophetic experience was true vision; and this seems worthy of credence in the light of the description of two visions in Sūra 53, together with a briefer reference in 81.19-24. The description is as follows:

Your companion neither went astray nor erred;
he expresses not mere fancies;

(the message) is indeed revelation revealed.
There taught him one of mighty power,
sound and steadfast; he stood straight
there on the highest horizon.
Then he came near and moved down—
two bow-lengths off or nearer—
and revealed to his servant what he revealed.
The heart falsified not what it saw;
dispute you with him what he sees?
He saw him also at a second descent
at the lote-tree of the limit,
where is the Garden of the Abode,
when the lote-tree was wondrously covered.
The eye wavered not nor exceeded.
He indeed from the signs of his Lord had sight of the greatest.
(53.2-18)

The speech of an honoured messenger is this,
strong, accredited with him of the throne,
obeyed, also trusty.
Not mad is your companion;
he verily saw him on the clear horizon,
and he is not suspected about the unseen. (81.19-24)

With regard to the second of the visions in Sūra 53 there is little to be said. Much discussion has led to no certain conclusions about 'the limit' and 'the Garden of the Abode'. All we know is that Muḥammad saw this supernatural figure and also saw something mysteriously covering a lote-tree; and this vision must have added to his subjective certainty. Two negative conclusions, however, are probably to be drawn from the passage. One is that Muḥammad had no further visions of this type up to the time of the revelation of the sūra; and the other is that the coming of revelations to Muḥammad was not normally accompanied by anything in the nature of a vision.

The first vision requires fuller consideration. Very significant is the word 'servant' (or 'slave'), *'abd,* in verse 10. Even those Muslim commentators who hold that all the revelations were brought by Gabriel admit that 'his servant' cannot mean 'Gabriel's servant' but must mean 'God's servant', since *'abd* is appropriate only of the relation to God. A few Muslim commentators conclude from this that the vision was a vision of God; and this must also be the conclusion of the Western scholar. Muḥammad, at least for a time, believed he had seen the supreme deity, and presumably still believed this when Sūra 53 was revealed. Later, especially when he learnt that Jews and Christians held that God cannot be seen, he came to think that the vision had been not of God but of an angel; in 6.103 it is asserted that 'sight reaches him (God) not'. The phrase about the signs of his Lord may have been added to make this clear, although the word *'abd* was left. Verse 10 can indeed be interpreted to mean 'the angel revealed something to God's servant', but this is too awkward to have been the original meaning. The words 'saw him on the clear horizon' in Sūra 81 are taken to refer to this first vision.

In this passage the words *waḥy* and *awḥā* are translated 'revelation' and 'revealed', since they eventually became the standard terms for the verbal revelations which were collected to form the Qur'ān. While what was revealed in the vision might conceivably be one of the two passages claimed as the earliest revelation, examination of the uses of this root shows that it originally had a much wider meaning than the later technical one of a revelation consisting of words. While in most instances the meaning approximates to the technical one, there are others where it is rather different, and this suggests that it may be only in the latest sūras that the word had exclusively the technical meaning. Some of these other uses may now be looked at.

An instructive verse is 19.11 which describes how Zacharias, after being rendered dumb, went out from the sanctuary 'and *awḥā* to his people that they should glorify (God) morning and evening'. This is, of course, reminiscent of *Luke* 1.22, where the Greek word is *dianeuōn,* which means 'nodding' or 'beckoning', that is, making signs with either the head or the hand. A translation such as 'signalled' could be used in the verse quoted. Richard Bell in his translation of the Qur'ān regularly uses 'suggests' which suits most of the instances, but it has psychological connotations which are not helpful. One of the translations given in Lane's *Lexicon* is 'put into his mind', and this comes near to the main meaning, but does not fit the verse about Zacharias. In pre-Islamic poetry *waḥy* means 'writing' and is often used of inscriptions on stone. Nöldeke-Schwally think the basic meaning is 'Andeutungen machen', that is to hint or to give intimations or indications, and, in addition to giving many references, they quote the phrase 'the *waḥy* of the eyes is their speech'.[3] Basically, then, *waḥy* is a form of communication but usually less precise than speech. The translation 'indicated' is sometimes useful.

In many cases what is communicated in *waḥy* is a command. God 'indicated' to Moses that he should go by night with the people and strike a way through the sea (20.77; cf. 26.52,63), and also that he should strike the rock with his staff to bring out water (7.160). Similarly to Noah God 'indicated' that he should make the ark *bi-a'yuni-nā wa-waḥyi-nā,* that is, probably, 'under our eyes and by our "indication''' (11.37; cf. 23.27). Muḥammad also is included here: 'We "indicated" to you that you should follow the religion of Abraham as a Ḥanīf' (16.123). The normal grammatical construction in these verses is the imperative preceded by the particle *an*, as if what the recipient was conscious of was simply the command. Sometimes, however, what is 'indicated' to Muḥammad is not a command but a verbal statement which seems to be other than the actual Qur'ān, though it could be a credal summary of Qur'ānic teaching.

> I am only a human being like you
> to whom it has been 'indicated' that your god is one God.
> (18.110; cf. 21.108; 41.6)

In these instances the recipients of *waḥy* are prophets or messengers, but in 16.68 we read: 'Your Lord "indicated" to the bee that she should take houses . . .'; while the account of the creation of the seven heavens in 41.12 contains the words: 'and "indicated" in respect of each heaven its *amr*', where *amr* presumably means the 'command' or law of its nature. These examples make it clear that *waḥy* was widely used in a non-technical way.

The conclusion to which all this points with a high degree of probability is that during the three-year period Muḥammad was indeed receiving *waḥy* but not in the form of verbal revelation. Towards the end of the period, however, the *waḥy* may sometimes have taken a verbal Qur'ānic form. As already mentioned, some such view as this is supported by the assertion that during the three years the angel coming to Muḥammad was not Gabriel but Isrāfīl.

For the view that at first Muḥammad received non-verbal *waḥy* the Qur'ān may be said to provide negative support in that everywhere in the Qur'ān some central features of Islam are assumed to be already in existence; or, in other words, Muḥammad had learnt many aspects of Islam before he received the first revelation recorded in the Qur'ān, whether it be Sūra 96 or some other. What Muḥammad learnt by this non-verbal *waḥy* would appear to comprise at least the four following matters.

Firstly, Muḥammad believed he had received a prophetic vocation from God. Although the story of Gabriel saying 'You are the Messenger of God' is to be rejected, it seems certain that Muḥammad was assured in some way that God had given him a prophetic vocation. How he expressed this in words is not clear; it is most likely that he first thought of himself as sent to 'warn' the people of Mecca (as will be seen in section 4). It is possible that this conviction of a prophetic vocation is what was 'revealed' to him in the first vision. On the other hand, various stories in the Sīra about his thinking of throwing himself down from a high rock suggest that it may only be over a period of time that his conviction of vocation became established. It is also possible that he did not at first think of the divine being who gave him his vocation as *Allāh,* since many of his contemporaries regarded *Allāh* as a high god, not as the unique God. It is noteworthy that in the earliest revelations the divine being is mostly called 'your Lord' (*rabbu-ka*) and not *Allāh,* and this would seem to imply that there was a special relationship between Muḥammad and God as a result of the giving of a vocation and its acceptance.

Secondly, in the verbal revelations it is always taken for granted that Muḥammad's 'Lord' is none other than God who is worshipped by Jews and Christians. In the Sīra Muḥammad was assured by Waraqa that his experiences were similar to those of Moses; and this, or some similar assurance, was undoubtedly of great importance for him. It is virtually certain that the verses '(your Lord) taught by the pen, taught people what they did not know' (96.4f.) refer to the Jewish and Christian scriptures. Though probably late Meccan, the verse 46.10 may also be relevant:

> Say: Have you considered?
> If it is from God and you have disbelieved in it,
> and a witness of the Israelites has witnessed
> to the like of it, and has believed (in that?),
> but you have been too proud . . .

The interpretation of this verse is much debated, but it might conceivably mean that Muḥammad had received some confirmation from a Jew that his revelations were similar to the Bible, even if this Jew did not become a Muslim. Apart from this last verse, however, it would seem that the belief that the revelations came from one who was also God for Jews and Christians must have been part of the non-verbal or non-Qur'ānic *waḥy.*

Thirdly, it appears that the 'prayer' or 'worship' (*ṣalāt*) was already being observed by Muḥammad before the first verbal revelation. Certainly *ṣalāt* is not commanded for Muḥammad in the Qur'ān, and a fairly early passage (96.9f.) speaks of an opponent stopping the *ṣalāt* of one of the Muslims. It may be that the precise form of the *ṣalāt* as it was observed in later times was only evolved gradually. In this case it is conceivable that the first five verses of Sūra 96 mark the introduction into the *ṣalāt* of the recitation of some part of the verbal *waḥy.*

Fourthly, in several of the earlier sūras the word *tazakkī* occurs, and has been found mysterious by commentators and translators. It combines the ideas of purification and almsgiving, and one translation is 'purification by almsgiving'. It is probably a way of describing the practical duties to be observed by the Muslims in the earliest period. The giving away of some part of their wealth as alms was doubtless an important part of this, especially in the light of the Qur'ānic critique of the wealthy Meccans. While *tazakkī* may be an early form of the duty of *zakāt,* it may also include other matters. The payment of *zakāt* and the observing of *ṣalāt* came to be the basic demand made of new converts to Islam, and this double requirement is frequently mentioned in the Qur'ān.

These considerations make it likely that many of the central features of Islam took shape in the period of non-verbal *waḥy* and before Muḥammad received any of the revelations now collected in the Qur'ān.

2 THE 'MANNERS' OF REVELATION

Muslim scholars of the Qur'ān studied a topic which they called 'the manners of revelation' (*kayfiyyāt al-waḥy*). Several of their 'manners' were based on Sīra-material, but something is also to be learned from the Qur'ān. It is convenient to use the terms 'revelation' and 'the receiving of revelation' to describe this experience, although these terms and their equivalents in other European languages have connotations which are sometimes foreign to the Qur'ān. It has already been seen that there is a non-technical use of the words *waḥy* and *awḥā,* and a distinction has been drawn between non-verbal and verbal revelation. The latter is what Muslim scholarship regarded as the norm, and its content is collected in the Qur'ān. The Qur'ān also uses another term for this, namely 'caused to come down' (*nazzala*; verbal noun *tanzīl*; also *anzala*). Before considering the manners of revelation, however, it will be convenient to look at the distinction between revelation and dreams.

It seems on the whole that this distinction is implied in the Qur'ān, but the matter is not entirely clear. For one thing, it is difficult to know how the ancient Arabs conceived of dreams. They presumably thought of them as real experiences, but perhaps not in our modern materialistic sense of 'real'. Further it has to be kept in mind that Qur'ānic Arabic does not clearly distinguish between 'sleep' and 'dream', using *nawm* for both, and also that *ru'ya,* which we translate 'vision', is only a kind of seeing. The word *aḥlām* (plural of *ḥulm*) is used for 'dreams' in 12.44 and 21.5, but these passages contribute nothing to the discussion, since the persons depicted as using the word do not believe that divine messages may come through dreams.

In a passage about Abraham and his son (37.102-5), the former says, 'O my son, I see while sleeping (or 'in a dream') that I sacrifice you'. Later in stopping the sacrifice God says, 'You counted true the vision'. Thus a prophet sees something in a dream which is tantamount to a command from God to act as he saw himself acting in the dream; and later he is praised for regarding this as a genuine message from God.

From Muḥammad's Medinan period two dreams of this type are recorded. One was just before the battle of Badr.

> God made you (Muḥammad) see them in your sleep as few;
> if he had made you see them as many,
> you (all) would have lost heart . . .

But the next verse (44) runs:

> When you met, God made you (all) see them as few in your eyes,
> and made you few in their eyes,
> that God might accomplish a matter already fixed . . .

It is implied that the Muslims acted in accordance with Muḥammad's dream, and that its effect is confirmed by the Muslims' waking experience of victory. In this dream only the seeing of something is mentioned, but in the other dream, about the time of al-Ḥudaybiya, seeing appears to be accompanied by the hearing of words: 'God gave his Messenger a true vision in reality, "You shall indeed enter the Sacred Mosque"' (48.27). Muḥammad seems to have organized the expedition to al-Ḥudaybiya primarily on the basis of this vision; so we must conclude that he and his contemporaries considered such a vision or dream as authoritative. Doubtless, however, good strategic reasons could also have been adduced.

There is a brief reference to a vision in 17.60:

> We said to you (Muḥammad)
> that your Lord has comprehended the people,
> and we made the vision we showed you
> only a test for the people.

This could perhaps be the vision at Badr just mentioned, or perhaps some vision otherwise unrecorded, or just conceivably the experience referred to in 17.1. This latter verse is:

> Praise be to him who took his servant by night
> from the Sacred Mosque to the Furthest Mosque,
> around which we have given blessing,
> so that we might show him of our signs . . .

This is the only Qur'ānic basis for the accounts of Muḥammad's night-journey (*isrā'*) and ascension (*mi'rāj*) into heaven, except perhaps for the phrase in the mouth of the unbelievers, who are not prepared to give credence to him 'until you ascend into heaven, nor to your ascent until you bring us down a writing'. Later biographies, of course, have long descriptions of these experiences. It seems best to regard 17.1 as describing an experience of Muḥammad's, which was of great importance for him, but did not yield any verbal revelation. If we may now generalize from this and the previous examples, it would seem that dreams and visions, though they may be the source of practical commands, do not give any theoretical or general statements suitable for inclusion in the Qur'ān. In the light of what was said above about the two early visions described in Sūra 53, where *waḥy* is clearly mentioned, it is possible that Muḥammad may have regarded these later visions as providing non-verbal *waḥy*.

The early passage 75.16-19 is a convenient starting-point for an examination of what the Qur'ān says about the 'manners of revelation':

> Do not move your tongue in it to hasten with it;
> ours it is to collect it and recite it.
> When we recite it, follow the reciting of it.
> After it is ours to explain it.

This appears to describe an experience in which Muḥammad heard God speaking, presumably without any visual accompaniments, and then himself recited the words he had heard and so memorized them. The word 'collect' (*jam'*) was later used for the work of the scholars under the caliph 'Uthmān in producing a complete and authoritative text. Here, however, it might refer to the bringing together of separately revealed passages so as to form sūras. Perhaps this experience of 'reciting after God' is also referred to in 87.6:

> We shall cause you to recite so that you forget not,
> except what God will.

A later, but probably still Meccan, passage has an important description of several different manners of revelation (42.51f.):

> It befitted not a man that God should address him
> except by *waḥy* or from behind a veil,
> or should send a messenger who would reveal what he will . . .
> Thus we revealed to you (Muḥammad) a spirit from our *amr*:
> unknown to you what the Book was, what faith was,
> but we made it a light,
> by which we guide whom we will of our servants.

The words translated 'reveal' are forms of *awḥā*, the verb corresponding to the noun *waḥy*. In this passage three or four different 'manners' seem to be distinguished: (a) address by *waḥy*; (b) address from behind a veil; (c) the sending of a messenger to 'reveal'; (d) the 'revealing' of a spirit. It is possible that these are not all different, but to begin with they have to be treated as such. The 'manner' already mentioned, following the reciting of God, would seem to be the second in this list, namely, address from behind a veil, since this implies hearing without seeing.

This may have been an early 'manner' which ceased to occur after the third 'manner' with Gabriel as the messenger came to be regarded as normal. There are a number of verses, however, in which God might be speaking from behind a veil, notably those to be considered in respect of the claim that the Qur'ān brings reports of events in the distant past (pp.65–7 below).

Since the first 'manner' opens the list, one would be justified in thinking that it refers to the two early visions described in Sūra 53, and that it means primarily non-verbal *waḥy*. It may also describe what was conveyed in the other visions and dreams discussed above. After the third 'manner', with Gabriel as the messenger, was taken to be the normal or standard one, Muslim scholars tended to read this back into early passages where the 'manner' was probably different. In the Meccan period, however, messengers other than Gabriel were spoken of. Sometimes there is mention of 'the spirit' by itself:

> The holy Spirit (*rūḥ al-qudus*) caused it to come down
> from your Lord with the truth. (16.102)

> It is the sending down (*tanzīl*) of the Lord of the Worlds,
> which the trusty Spirit has brought down on your heart,
> that you may be of those warning. (26.192–4)

Probably the 'noble messenger' of 81.19 is to be taken as the Spirit. In other passages, however, angels accompany the Spirit in bringing down the message:

> He sends down the angels with the Spirit from his *amr*
> upon whom he will of his servants. (16.2)

> There come down the angels and the Spirit in (that night)
> by permission of their Lord from (about?) every *amr*. (97.4)

Yet again the angels are mentioned by themselves:

> We send not down the angels but with the truth. (15.8)

> We (the angels) do not come down
> except by the command (*amr*) of your Lord. (19.64)

In the last verse the angels must be speaking in their own name, though presumably by God's command. Finally, Jibrīl or Gabriel is named as messenger:

> Gabriel caused it to come down
> on your heart by God's permission. (2.97)

When this last was accepted as normal by later Muslims, the Spirit was identified with Gabriel, though there is no direct evidence for this in the Qur'ān. In most of these passages the verb is *nazzala*.

The fourth 'manner' (42.52) is the most puzzling, although there is a similar phrase in 40.15:

> He casts the Spirit from his *amr*
> upon whom he will of his servants
> that he may warn of the day of meeting.

Whereas in 42.52 'a Spirit from God's *amr*' was revealed to Muḥammad, here 'the Spirit from his *amr*' is cast upon the prophet. In either case it would seem that the Spirit is received by the prophet into himself in some sense. This appears to be different from the function of the holy Spirit or the trusty Spirit as a messenger. There is also some mystery about *amr*. The Arabic word may mean 'command' or 'affair', but neither of these alternatives gives a wholly satisfactory sense, and it has been suggested that *amr* has here some of the connotations of the Jewish *memrā* or 'word' of God.[4]

It should be noted that another root *shara'a* may sometimes have the meaning of 'revealed'. Because in modern times the word *sharī'a* means almost exclusively 'Islamic law', it is frequently supposed that this word and cognate ones like *shar'* and *shar'ī* must always be translated 'law' and 'legal'. This supposition is erroneous. Careful reading of medieval texts will produce passages where only 'revelation' and 'revelational' give a satisfactory rendering. This is particularly the case with *shar'*, but even *sharī'a* is found in passages where 'law' makes no sense; e.g. al-Mas'ūdī (d.956) writes 'what we have mentioned of the reports of the beginning of creation is what the *sharī'a* brought and one generation related to its successors', where *sharī'a* must be 'revelation' or 'revealed scriptures', since reports of the beginning of creation have nothing to do with law.[5]

It is worth considering whether *shara'a* and its derivatives are ever used for 'revelation' in the Qur'ān. The primary use of the root seems to be of animals going or being driven to water, but the connotation of gaining access is prominent, and the idea of 'access' or 'opening' is dominant in some of the derivatives. Thus 5.48 runs: 'For each of you (Jews, Christians, Muslims) we have set a *shir'a* and a plain *minhāj*', where this last word can only mean 'road' or 'path'. Several commentators say that *shir'a* means *sharī'a*, which could mean 'law'; but it is more likely to be non-technical here and parallel to *minhāj*, so that it means something like 'way of access (to religious truth)' or 'revealed way of life'. The same can be said of *sharī'a* in 45.18: 'then we set you upon a *sharī'a* of the *amr* (affair?), so follow it'. Finally in 42.13 it is stated that God '*shara'a* to you (Muslims) in religion what he enjoined on Noah'; and verse 21 is similar. A common interpretation is 'instituted', but something non-technical is preferable; Richard Bell translated 'made accessible', but 'revealed' might also be possible. In this case as in others the Qur'ān takes a word of general meaning and uses it in a special way. The idea expressed is at first indefinite, but it gradually becomes more definite, and as it does so the word in question tends to be restricted to its technical meaning.

The conclusion to be drawn from this examination of words is that the experience of revelation was not of a single type, but varied from time to time, even if latterly it came near to a single norm. This is the simplest way of accounting for the wide variations in the Qur'ānic language in respect of this matter. Despite this variety, however, the experience was always basically the same, namely, a communication from God to men with Muḥammad as intermediary.

The Qur'ān asserts its unique character as coming from God, and also claims that this is obvious to those who look carefully. In later centuries this was developed into the doctrine of the *i'jāz* of the Qur'ān, its inimitability or miraculous character. The inimitability is clearly stated in 17.88:

> Say: If humankind and the jinn joined together
> to bring the like of ths Qur'ān,
> they would not bring the like of it,
> even though one supported the other.

There are also challenges to Muḥammad's opponents to produce something like it, either a *ḥadīth* or discourse (52.34), or a sūra (2.23; 10.38) or ten sūras (11.13). It may be asked, however, whether this inimitability is based chiefly on its form or on its content. One verse (28.49) challenges the opponents to 'bring a book from God with better guidance than (the books of Moses), and then he (Muḥammad) will follow it', and this suggests that the main emphasis is on the teaching or content. Yet in other contexts, such as those about to be discussed, the emphasis may be more on the form.

Among the material in the Qur'ān, though not in the earliest passages, there are reports or stories about past events; and in respect of these the question is raised whether the Qur'ān is a source of historical knowledge independently of other sources. Muslims claim, for example, that the Qur'ānic denial of the crucifixion of Jesus is to be preferred to the New Testament version because it is an independent and superior historical source.

It is worth looking at some of the actual statements of the Qur'ān relevant to this point. At the end of three stories about former 'prophets', namely, Zacharias (the brother-in-law of Mary), Noah and Joseph, there come such statements as: 'That is from the reports of the unseen; we reveal it to you, although you were not present with them'

(3.44; cf. 11.49; 12.102). The phrase 'reports of the unseen' (*anbā' al-ghayb*) occurs only in these three verses, but there are several others which mention 'reports' (*anbā'*) as coming from God. In five of these God, speaking to Muḥammad, says 'we relate to you' (*naquṣṣu 'alay-ka*)—reports of the towns destroyed (7.101; 11.100), of the messengers (11.120), of the Seven Sleepers (18.13), and 'of what was before' (in fact, the story of Moses) (20.99). In one verse God says 'we recite to you the report of Moses' (28.3). This same verb is twice used similarly with the noun *āyāt*, 'signs' or 'verses': 'that we recite to you of the *āyāt* and the wise reminder' (3.58); 'these are of the *āyāt* of God, we recite them to you in truth' (2.252). It is significant here that there is no clear distinction between *awḥā* and these other words. The word *ghayb*, as used with *awḥā* and *anbā'*, does not appear to have any technical religious sense, but only to mean what is absent, unseen or unknown. In 3.44 and 12.102 it is followed by the words 'you were not present when . . .', and in 11.49 by 'it was unknown to you and your people before this'. It would seem that we are dealing with revelation even when the word is *qaṣṣa* (relate) or *talā* (recite).

The Muslim claim that such verses constitute an independent historical source is not acceptable to Western scholarship; but it is possible to suggest an alternative interpretation of the relevant phrases. This is based on the fact that at several points the Qur'ān describes as the direct action of God what is normally regarded as happening through a human agent. A verse (8.17) referring to the death of many pagan Meccans at Badr runs:

> You (Muslims) killed them not, God killed them;
> and you (Muḥammad) shot not when you shot, God shot.

The word *ramayta* here is probably to be taken of shooting arrows,[6] but, whatever the interpretation, it is implied that the actions of Muḥammad and his followers are in some sense God's actions. Similarly in 96.4f. it is stated that God 'taught people by the pen what they did not know', though this is to be taken as referring to previous scriptures and to pens wielded by human scribes.

If human actions can thus be regarded as essentially the actions of God, may it not be the case that, where the Qur'ān states that God revealed things to Muḥammad, there were also human intermediaries? There are strong grounds for holding that he himself had not read any Jewish or Christian scriptures, but, apart from what was common knowledge in Mecca, he probably had oral sources for many Biblical stories. There are thus two possible meanings for such a verse as 'we relate to you their report' (18.13). It may mean that God relates this story to Muḥammad by the mediation of other men, just as he taught people by the mediation of the pen of the scribe. Or it may mean that he taught Muḥammad directly. From an Arab standpoint the two interpretations are perhaps not so distinct as they appear to the Western scholar. God may relate to Muḥammad in revelation in an original and distinctive form what He as already related to him in a general way by a human intermediary. Both the precise form of the Qur'ānic verses and the meaning given to the story (for example, God's protection of prophets) come by revelation as usually understood, but the previous acquaintance with the stories also comes from God. With the human intermediary, however, the possibility of error comes in. If this way of interpreting is correct, it implies that the Qur'ān does not claim to be an independent historical source superior to other sources because of its divine origin.

Finally it should be mentioned that some modern Western scholars would hold that, whatever the 'manner' of revelation as experienced by the prophet, the messages he received came in fact from his unconscious (in a Jungian sense), partly from the personal unconscious and partly from the collective unconscious. At first sight this appears to be completely different from the standard Islamic view that the Qur'ān was mostly brought down from God to Muḥammad by Gabriel. Yet the difference is perhaps not so great as it appears, if one remembers that in dealing with religious matters the language used is picture-language or, as it might also be called 'iconic' language. An icon is a two-dimensional representation of a three-dimensional object, that is, one which is known not to be a full and complete representation and which only suggests the object. In the same way picture-language or iconic language is a knowingly inadequate representation of an object, and is strictly speaking not descriptive but only evocative. An angel is something like a human being but basically invisible and incorporeal (without a material physical body and its limitations), though it may sometimes assume a human form, perhaps with wings. All this is to suggest or evoke an idea of a reality which we cannot fully comprehend. Of the role of the angel in revelation we can say that its functioning is like that of a human intelligence, but that it is a reality other than the prophet.

The conception of the unconscious, even if it is restricted to the Jungian form, is still somewhat vague and has not yet acquired an established place in a general world-view. It seems to include the dynamism or life-energy which drives a person forward in living, but which is at the same time distinct from the person. The word 'unconscious' is also picture-language, evocative of something like a human consciousness and intelligence, though beyond the awareness of the individual. Jung distinguished a personal and a collective unconscious, the latter being what the individual shares with the society and culture to which he belongs. If we say that a 'revealed' message comes from the unconscious, that tells us little about its ultimate source, but to some extent it explains how the message is adapted to the recipient's thought-world and that of the community to which he belongs, since the unconscious somehow shares in these. Christians believe that God works in and through individuals in that manifestation of God which is the Holy Spirit, and this makes it possible for them to say that some of what comes to them from the unconscious, such as injunctions to act in a particular way, is ultimately from God. If this injunction or some religious assertion comes into a person's mind as a kind of inner prompting whose source is unknown to him, he may decide that this is divine guidance and follow it. If he further believes that it came through an angel, this seems to add hardly anything to the statement that it is divine guidance, though it may give greater subjective certainty. Whether it is really divine guidance or not does not depend on the 'manner' in which it came to him but on the quality of its 'fruits' (as was stated in ch. 1).

To say that in Muḥammad's case the revealed mesages came to him from his unconscious does not mean that they did not come from God, since God can work through created beings (angels, men, women), and so can presumably work through the personal or collective unconscious of a created human being. Such a view makes it easier to understand how the revealed messages were adapted to the outlook of their first audience in Mecca. Moreover, it does not really contradict the assertion that Muḥammad experienced the messages as coming through an angel, since that is picture-language for a reality known mainly through its effects. In any case the experienced 'manner' of revelation is not a guarantee of genuineness, since Muḥammad at first thought the 'satanic verses' were genuine. It is the 'fruits' which are the ultimate criterion of genuineness.

3 THE COLLECTION AND REVISION OF THE QUR'ĀN

Modern scholars, and notably Richard Bell, have argued that careful examination of the text of the Qur'ān brings to light many examples of revision.[7] The type of revision for which it is easiest to give evidence is the addition of words, phrases or whole verses; but there are also other types. Even if three-quarters of the instances of revision indicated by Bell are rejected, there is still an enormous amount of revision. The aim of the present section is not to consider details, but to see whether the Qur'ān itself shows how such revision might come about. Even if Muslims reject the word 'revision', there is still the problem of how the text of the Qur'ān, with its many awkward features, came to have its present form. This may also be called the problem of the 'collection' of the Qur'ān.

As a preliminary it may be definitely stated that the Qur'ān does not countenance any revision of the text by Muḥammad *of his own volition*.

> When our verses are recited to them as evidences,
> those who look to no meeting with us, say,
> Bring a Qur'ān other than this, or alter it.
> Say, It is not for me to alter it of my own accord;
> I follow only what is revealed to me;
> if I disobey my Lord, I fear the punishment of a mighty day. (10.15)

The punishment for falsely alleging that something has been revealed is described even more vividly in 69.44–7:

> If he were to forge against us any statements,
> we would take him by the right hand,
> then cut away his heart-vein;
> not one of you would protect him.

There is also some material to show that the pagan Meccans brought pressure to bear on Muḥammad to get him to compromise in some way, probably by departing from strict monotheism.

> They almost seduced you from what we revealed to you,
> so that you invented against us something other,
> then they would have taken you as a friend.
> Had we not established you (Muḥammad),
> you had almost inclined to them some little.
> Then we would have made you taste the double of living
> and the double of dying;
> and you would not have found any helper against us. (17.73–5)

Such verses could, of course, be regarded as a deliberate attempt to deceive people, but any such hypothesis is to be rejected, since it makes nonsense of the career of Muḥammad. We take it, then, that Muḥammad was convinced that any attempt on his part to produce revelations or to revise earlier revelations would have disastrous consequences for himself.

It is next to be noted, however, that in one or two passages the Qur'ān envisages the possibility that Muḥammad may forget certain verses; and this, of course, is tantamount to revision by omission or deletion, even though the forgetting is caused by God. Incidentally, this implies that the revelations were not written down. One such passage is:

> We shall cause you to recite, and you shall not forget,
> except what God wills . . . (87.6f.)

Another passage probably refers to the forgetting of revelation, though it might conceivably refer rather to other facts connected with revelation:

> . . . and remember your Lord when you forget, and say:
> Perhaps my Lord will guide (*yahdiya*) me
> to something nearer true guidance (*rashad*) than this. (18.24)

The reference to revelation is clear in the following:

> Wherever we cancel a verse or cause its forgetting
> we bring a better than it or the like of it. (2.106)

Thus within revelation there may occur the deletion of certain verses and the substitution of others for them.

In the last quotation the verb *nansakh* has been translated 'cancel', though the root later provided the technical term for 'abrogation', *naskh.* The standard view among Muslims is that a verse with a command is abrogated when, owing to a change of circumstances, the command has no longer to be carried out; but the abrogated verses are retained as part of the Qur'ān. Abrogation is thus a kind of revision, but not the kind being discussed here. The same verb in the form *yansakhu* occurs in the verse on which the story of the so-called satanic verses is based (to be discussed in the next chapter). Here (22.52) it is stated that 'God cancels what Satan throws in, then God adjusts his *āyāt*' (signs or verses). The translation 'cancels' is necessary here, since the supposedly interpolated verses are not included in the Qur'ān; and this justifies the translation 'cancel' in 2.106.

A number of other verses speak of the cancellation or replacement of part of the revelation:

> God will efface (*yamḥū*) what he will, or establish;
> and with him is the 'mother' of the book. (13.37)

> When we put an *āya* in the place of another—
> and God knows best what he sends down—
> they say, You (Muḥammad) are only an inventor;
> rather, most of them do not know. (16.101)

> We have made changes (*ṣarrafnā*) in this Qur'ān
> that they might be reminded. (17.41)

> If we will, we shall indeed take away
> what we have revealed to you. (17.86)

In the last two verses the translation or interpretation may be disputed, but apart from these there is sufficient evidence to show that the Qur'ān sanctions something more radical than abrogation in the technical sense (where the abrogated verses are retained in the Qur'ān); it speaks of the removal of verses which had once been part of the Qur'ān, either by simple deletion or by the substitution of others for them.

It is important to look at the question of revision in the context of the 'collection' (*jam'*) of the Qur'ān. The fundamental passage is 75.17f. (quoted on p.62), where God addressing Muḥammad says: 'Ours it is to collect it and recite it; when we recite it, follow the reciting of it'. It is widely held by both Muslim and Western scholars that, although some of the shorter sūras may have constituted a single revelation, many of the revelations came as passages much shorter than a sūra. The collecting, then, probably means the bringing together of short passages revealed on separate occasions, and the forming of these into sūras. From the challenges to opponents to produce something like the Qur'ān (see p.65) it may be deduced that some sūras were already in existence. God's collecting or bringing together of several short passages must then have been recited as a whole to Muḥammad according to one or other of the 'manners'; and thus Muḥammad would believe that anything he did under the head of 'collecting' was revealed to him by God.

The operation of collecting, too, would be an opportunity for making adjustments, so that the passages fitted together better or in order to secure some other end. The Qur'ān, in fact, uses a word which can be translated 'adjust' in a sense which is tantamount to revision. The word is *aḥkama,* with its passive participle *muḥkama.* Its primary meaning is 'make firm' or 'construct well' (as of a building). In the four instances of the word in the Qur'ān it is possible that it refers to this process of putting together separate revelations, perhaps with some changes. Three instances deal with *āyāt,* 'signs' or 'verses', and one with a sūra:

> A book whose *āyāt* are adjusted. (11.1)
>
> Then God adjusts his *āyāt.* (22.52)
>
> When an adjusted sūra is sent down . . . (47.20)
>
> It is he who sent down to you the book;
> in it are *āyāt* adjusted, which are the 'mother' of the book,
> and others 'resembling' (*mutashābihāt*);
> and those with deviation in their hearts
> follow what 'resembles' of it,
> desiring dissension and desiring its interpretation,
> though none save God knows its interpretation. (3.7)

The first three of these instances, when understood of the process of collecting and revising, make good sense. The fourth is more difficult, since the distinction between *muḥkamāt* and *mutashābihāt* has been so much discussed that it is hard to know the original meaning of the verse. The verb *tashābaha* elsewhere in the Qur'ān means 'to resemble one another' or 'to be like'. There are many verses in the Qur'ān which closely resemble one another, and indeed are sometimes identical; and sometimes the contexts are different and may give a different nuance to resembling verses. If at one time, too, all the separate revelations existed as separate passages which could be recited in any order, there were many possibilities of confusion. Perhaps some opponents at Medina had caused trouble by making an unauthorized selection of passages which altered the meaning slightly. The hypothesis of 'adjustment' is attractive and might show another aspect of the process of collecting. Certainly the Qur'ān itself fully admits the possibility of some revision of its text, and this admission would probably cover all that Richard Bell intended.

4 THE CONCEPTION OF THE PROPHETIC VOCATION

In Arabic Muḥammad is mostly called *rasūl Allāh,* the messenger or apostle of God, whereas in English he is rather spoken of as a prophet. Several other words are also used in the Qur'ān, notably *nadhīr* (warner), *bashīr* (bringer of good tidings), *mudhakkir* (admonisher or warner), as well as *nabī* (prophet). These terms express different aspects of the vocation of Muḥammad. *Nadhīr* appears to be the earliest and *rasūl* the latest, and then *rasūl* comes to comprise what was expressed by the earlier terms and to add new functions appropriate to Muḥammad's position in Medina.

The most frequent term in the earlier passages of the Qur'ān is *nadhīr,* together with its participial form *mundhir* and the verb *andhara.* As was noted above, the verb is used in the very early phrase 'rise and warn' (74.2), which is a command appropriate to the beginning of Muḥammad's public preaching. The words 'warn' and 'warner' are sometimes used in this way without stating what is being warned against, but other passages make it clear that people are being warned that they will have to appear before God's judgement-seat on the Last Day and may be in danger of receiving punishment. This is implied in a verse following the one quoted: 'the Wrath (or punishment) flee' (74.5).[8] There is a clear statement in 78.40: 'we warn you of a punishment near'; while in 92.14 the warning is of 'a fire blazing', that is, Hell. Muḥammad's vocation is described in 36.3–6:

> You are of those sent (*mursalīn*)
> on a straight path—
> a revelation from the Sublime, the Merciful—
> to warn a people whose fathers were not warned.

The warner is sent to a whole *qawm* (tribe or people) or *umma* (community), not to individuals, though the response hoped for is individual rather than communal. Moreover nearly every people has had a warner sent to it:

> There was no community but a warner came among them. (35.22)

The one exception is apparently Mecca, as in 36.6 above and in the following verses:

> We bestowed on them no book to study
> and before you sent no warner. (34.44)

> (The book sent down) is the truth from your Lord,
> that you (Muḥammad) might warn a people
> to whom before you no warner has come. (34.3; cf. 28.46)

The people to whom no warner has come is presumably Quraysh, and perhaps some of the surrounding tribes. It is implied, at least in later passages of the Qur'ān, especially 2.125–8, that after Abraham had established the Ka'ba and the pilgrimage rites, there was for a time at Mecca a community of his descendants and perhaps others which followed his teaching; but this community had at some point disappeared. Muḥammad's vocation as a warner is specially directed to Mecca and its suroundings:

> Thus we revealed to you an Arabic *qur'ān*,
> that you may warn the Mother of Towns and those round it,
> warn of the day of assembling, of which is no doubt—
> a party in the Garden and a party in the Fire. (42.7; cf. 6.92)

Although Muḥammad's original vocation was to warn Mecca and the region round, it should be noted that, even before the Hijra, his vocation was spoken of as universal. The following verses are in Blachère's order of dating:

> We have sent you as a mercy to the worlds. (21.107)

> ... to the worlds a warner. (25.1)

> We have sent you to humankind altogether
> as bringer of good tidings and warner. (34.28)

> Say: O humankind, I am the messenger of God to you all. (7.158)

> We have sent you to humankind as a messenger. (4.79)

Prominent as warnings of the Last Day are in early passages, there are also many references to God's 'signs' (*āyāt*), that is, evidences in nature of his benevolence towards the human race and of his power. Before long the vocation of the 'bringer of good tidings' (*bashīr*) is combined with that of the warner; and the participial form *mubashshir* and the verb *bashshara* also occur. The verb is indeed used in a neutral sense in the phrase (which is found seven times) 'announce to them a painful punishment' (84.24; etc.). When combined with *nadhīr,* however, the *bashīr* is the bearer of good news, presumably the more positive aspects of Qur'ānic teaching.

> O prophet, we have sent you as a witness (*shāhid*)
> and a bringer of good tidings and a warner,
> and a summoner to God by his leave, and a shining lamp;
> give good tidings to the believers
> that theirs is great bounty from God. (33.45–7)

This justifies a positive interpretation of 19.97:

> We make it easy in your (Arabic) tongue,
> only that thereby you may bring good tidings to the devout
> and thereby may warn a contentious people.

The participle *mudhakkir* occurs only once, and the translation 'warner' would be suitable; it is in a passage (88.21f.) where Muḥammad is told: 'Warn them, you are only a warner; you are not a controller over them'. The corresponding imperative *dhakkir,* however, occurs seven times (as at the beginning of the quotation), and there are over sixty instances of the passive *dhukkira,* together with the form *tadhakkara,* which has much the same meaning as the passive. In addition the related nouns *dhikr, dhikrā* and *tadhkira* are found frequently, and often mean something like 'warning'. The basic meaning of the root is 'to remember', and *dhikr* is properly 'remembrance'; but from this the meaning spreads out considerably. Thus 87.15 could be translated 'remembers the name of his Lord and prays', but it seems rather to mean 'mentions the name of his Lord and prays'; and in later times *dhikr* came to designate a form of worship among Sufis which could consist entirely in the repetition of the name of God. For the verb *dhakkara,* which is basically 'to cause to remember' or 'to remind', Lane gives the following extended meanings: 'He exhorted; admonished; exhorted to obedience; gave good advice, and reminded of the results of affairs; reminded of what might soften the heart, by the mention of rewards and punishments'.[9] In many of the instances in the Qur'ān the translation 'warn' is appropriate, but 'admonish' may be used to differentiate from *andhara*; and for *dhukkira* and *tadhakkara,* instead of 'were warned' one can say 'accepted the admonition (and acted accordingly)'. The nouns *dhikrā* and *tadhkira* usually mean 'warning'; and the same seems to be true of most of the instances of *dhikr,* though it can also mean 'remembrance' as in 12.42: 'The devil caused him (Joseph) to forget the remembrance of his Lord'.

The connection of all these words with revelation and the Last Day is often clearly shown:

> So admonish; the admonition (*dhikrā*) indeed avails.
> He who fears will accept the admonition,
> but the most wretched will turn from it,
> he who burns in the great Fire. (87.9–12)

> How, when the Hour has come upon them,
> shall they have their warning (*dhikrā*)? (47.18)

> Admonish by the Qur'ān him who fears my threat. (50.45)

> (Opponents say:) Has the *dhikr* been sent down
> to him (alone) among us?
> But they are in doubt of my *dhikr*,
> but they have not yet tasted my punishment. (38.8)

> We gave Moses and Aaron the criterion
> and a light and a *dhikr* . . .
> This is a blessed *dhikr* we have sent down;
> are you then rejecting it? (21.48,50)

The word *nabī*, 'prophet', which does not occur at all in Blachère's first Meccan period, has a completely different emphasis. It has been borrowed by Arabic, probably from Jewish Aramaic, but was in use before the time of Muḥammad.[10] In the Qur'ān it is never used of Arabian prophets like Ṣāliḥ and Hūd, but only of Biblical personages. In Sūra 19, Jesus, Abraham, Isaac, Jacob, Moses, Ishmael and Idrīs (Enoch) are named as prophets; and then it is said (v.58): 'These are they God favoured of the prophets of the seed of Adam, and of those we carried with Noah, and of the seed of Abraham and Israel, and of those we guided and chose'. In 45.16 it is stated that 'we gave the Israelites the book, jurisdiction and prophethood (*nubuwwa*)'. There are over seventy instances of *nabī* and its plural forms in the Qur'ān, and most of these refer to Old Testament figures. One or two instances are more general, such as 43.6: 'How many a prophet we sent (*arsalnā*) to those of old!' The sending of prophets generally is mentioned in 7.94, while in 39.69 they appear on the Last Day, presumably as witnesses.

The remaining instances, mostly in late passages, refer to Muḥammad, usually as a prophet standing in the line of Old Testament prophets. Thus in 33.7 God is said to have exacted an agreement or pledge from various prophets, 'from you (Muḥammad), and from Noah and Abraham and Moses and Jesus son of Mary'. Another passage (4.163–5) may be quoted in full since it raises further points:

We revealed to you (Muḥammad),
as we revealed to Noah and the prophets after him,
and revealed to Abraham, Ishmael, Isaac, Jacob and the tribes,
and Jesus, Job, Jonah, Aaron and Solomon,
and to David we gave psalms—
and messengers we have told you of before,
and messengers we have not told you of;
and God addressed Moses directly—
messengers, bringers of good tidings and warnings,
that humankind might have no argument against God
after the messengers.

Apart from linking Muḥammad with the prophets of Israel, the passage identifies prophets and messengers, though perhaps the messengers were those outside the Biblical tradition, at least originally. The conception of the messengers, however, then subsumes the emphasis in the terms *bashīr* and *nadhīr* by speaking of the messengers as bringers of good tidings and warnings' (*mubashshirīn, mundhirīn*). It is in relation to the prophets of Israel that two phrases are to be understood, as applied to Muḥammad. To say he is 'the *ummī* prophet' (7.157f., quoted on p.53) means that he is similar to the Old Testament prophets but is non-Jewish; and to say that he is 'the seal of the prophets' (*khātam an-nabiyyīn*; 33.40) originally meant that the revelations he received confirmed those of the Biblical prophets before him, though Muslims now take it to mean that he was the last of the prophets and that no more are to be expected. In some late sūras (such as 66.1,9) the form of address 'O prophet' is used, though there is no reference to Jews in the context, thus implying that 'prophet' had become a standard description.

The word *rasūl*, 'messenger' or 'apostle', is probably not used in its later technical sense during the first Meccan period, though it occurs five times. In one verse (91.13) the person sent to Thamūd is called *rasūl Allāh*, while in 69.10 Pharaoh and other unbelievers are said to have 'disobeyed the messenger of their Lord'. Pharaoh's mesenger, again unnamed, is mentioned in 73.15,16 and, slightly later, in 44.17, while still later Moses and Aaron tell Pharaoh 'we are the messengers of your Lord' (20.47), and 'we are the messengers of the Lord of the worlds' (26.16). In 51.52, 44.13 and 20.134 a messenger is sent to unnamed unbelievers, though the Meccans seem to be intended, as is also the case in 73.15: 'We have sent to you a messenger as witness against you, as we sent to Pharaoh'. The prominence of Pharaoh in these early passages must have some significance. It may be that the messenger was not giving Pharaoh a scripture in any sense, but only a command to let the Israelites go (cf. 20.47). The messenger to Thamūd in 91.13 also had only a command for them. This suggestion gains some support from 72.23 where Muḥammad is told to say:

> (For me) is only the conveying (of truth) from God and of his message (*risāla*);
> he who disobeys God and his messenger,
> for him is the fire of Hell, to be there for ever.

The emphasis is on disobedience rather than unbelief.

What is apparently the earliest passage of all has not yet been mentioned, because its interpretation presents some difficulties. As a defence of the truth of the revelation it is stated that 'it is the speech of an honoured messenger' (81.19), and the messenger is commonly taken to be Gabriel. This interpretation is virtually impossible, however, since only much later is Gabriel named as the bearer of revelation, and before that there are usually several bearers, such as the angels and the Spirit (cf. p.63). Richard Bell holds that the passage containing 81.19 has been revised by the addition of verses 20, 21 to make it refer to Gabriel, but that originally it referred to Muḥammad himself. There is much to be said for this view since the same phrase is used of Muḥammad himself in 69.40, *rasūl karīm,* and also of a human messenger to Pharaoh in 44.17. Whatever the interpretation, however, *rasūl* in this verse can hardly have its full technical meaning.

While *rasūl* may originally have had the connotation of one who brought a command rather than a scripture and who was to be obeyed rather than believed, it soon came to incorporate the distinctive emphases of the other terms and to go beyond them, as can be seen in 4.165 (on p.76). The verb 'sent' (*arsala*) was indeed sometimes used with the other terms, as may be noticed in the quotations given earlier, but there is nothing technical there. The verb *arsala* never came to be restricted to God's sending of individuals, since it continued to have its secular uses (as in 12.19 where the members of a caravan *sent* a man to fetch water). The participle *mursalīn,* however, is used in a similar sense to *rasūl*; thus 6.48 runs: 'We send not the *mursalīn* save as *mubashshirīn* and *mundhirīn*'. Besides warning and bringing good tidings the *rasūl* like the *nabī* confirms previous revelations. This was the point of the statement that Muḥammad was not 'something new' (*bid'*) among the messengers (46.9). The essential message is made clear in 20.25: 'We sent no *rasūl* before you without our "indicating" to him that there is no deity save me, so worship me'. (For the sake of those who do not know Arabic it should be pointed out that there is no connection in Arabic between the words translated 'sent' and 'sent down'; one is *arsala,* and the other is *nazzala* or *anzala.*)

Further functions, however, came to be assigned to the *rasūl,* some at

Mecca, others after the Hijra to Medina. From an early period he is spoken of as a witness, though what is involved in this is not made clear. In 73.15 it is said to the unbelievers in Mecca: 'We have sent you a *rasūl* as a witness against you". The word used is *shāhid*; and the same word is applied to Muḥammad in 33.45 and 48.8 but without any hint of what he is to witness about. It seems likely that the witnessing was to be on the Last Day, since there are verses about the Last Day in which the word *shahīd* appears, presumably with the meaning of 'witness':

> We have appointed you (Muslims) a middle community
> to be witnesses against humankind,
> and the *rasūl* to be a witness against you. (2.143)

> How will it be when we bring from each community a witness,
> and bring you (Muḥammad) to be a witness
> against these (unbelievers)? (4.41)

> On the day we raise in each community
> of themselves a witness against them,
> and bring you (Muḥammad) as witness against these. (16.89)

> For every community is a *rasūl*,
> and when their *rasūl* comes (on the Last Day)
> it will be judged between them fairly
> and they will not be wronged. (10.47)

These quotations still do not make it clear what the witnessing is about, since all people's acts are recorded in a book. Al-Bayḍāwī in his comment on 2.143 suggests that communities will complain that they received no message, and the prophets will then appear to contradict this. This may be what was intended, since it is in line with the description of how on the Last Day the angels which had been regarded as pagan deities will deny that they had asked for worship and will repudiate their worshippers (see 19.82; 46.5f.).

It became a doctrine of later Islam that Muḥammad would intercede for sinners of his community on the Last Day, though this is not explicitly stated in the Qur'ān. Pre-Islamic pagans had held that the lesser deities (sometimes regarded as angels) were able in this life to intercede on their behalf with the high god. The Qur'ān shows awareness of this, but denies that the deities or angels have any power of intercession (deities—43.86; 36.23; angels—53.26; 21.28). On the other hand, it is implied that God may grant the power of intercession in some cases. Angels might be thought of in the first place (cf. 34.23), but the following verses could apply to human beings:

> They will have no power of intercession,
> except him who has with his Lord a covenant (*'ahd*). (19.87)

There is no intercessor except after his permission. (10.3)

Who is he who interceded with God
except by his permission? (2.255)

In the context of 19.87 the pagan deities are referred to, but the mention of a covenant might connect with God's covenant (*mīthāq*) with the prophets of Israel in 3.81. In the end, then, the Qur'ān may be said to be favourable to regarding intercession on the Last Day as part of the function of the *rasūl* (or of the prophet—39.69), but it does not explicitly say this is so.

Once Muḥammad was settled in Medina it became part of his function to decide disputes between Muslims, and this is clearly stated:

O believers, obey God
and obey the *rasūl* and those of you in authority;
if you dispute over anything, refer it to God and the *rasūl*,
if you are believing in God and the Last Day. (4.59)

We sent down to you (Muḥammad) the book and the truth,
that you might judge between people
by what God showed you. (4.105)

Those (prophets of Israel) are they to whom we gave
the book and jurisdiction (*ḥukm*) and prophethood.
(6.89; cf. 3.79)

In 5.42 Muḥammad is told that, if the Jews come to him for a decision and he agrees to give one, he is to 'judge between them justly'. It can only have been in Medina, of course, that this function of the *rasūl* emerged. (The statement in *Muḥammad at Medina*, 229, that it was already found in Mecca was based on an interpretation of 10.47 which I now realize to be erroneous; Rudi Paret's comparative studies make it certain that 10.47 is to be taken eschatologically.)

Finally there is the question of what the prophet or messenger was thought of as receiving in revelation. In 2.151 it is stated that '. . . we sent among you a messenger, one of you, reciting to you our *āyāt*, appointing you *zakāt*, and teaching you the book and the wisdom'. This verse contains two of the terms which Richard Bell studied under the heading of 'names of the revealed message', namely *āyāt* and book.[11] The word *āyāt* means both 'signs' and 'verses'. In many of the Meccan sūras there are passages which may be described as *āyāt* since they speak of 'signs' of God's goodness and power in natural phenomena. These may well have had an independent existence of some sort before being collected into sūras, and that may explain their mention in this verse. A second name, *mathānī*, is obscure and may be left aside here, though the statement in 15.87 that Muḥammad has received 'seven of the *mathānī* and the mighty Qur'ān' shows it was something which came to messengers.

The most important question is whether there is a distinction between other two terms, Qur'ān and Book. Bell held that from an early point in his prophetic career, though not from the beginning, Muḥammad thought of the separate revelations he was receiving as constituting a single Qur'ān. After he had been a year or two in Medina, however, he thought of them as constituting 'the Book' which it was his task to produce. In Sūra 19 the phrase 'in the Book mention . . .' is found several times, followed by the names of Mary, Abraham, Moses, Ishmael, Idrīs (vv. 16, 41, 51, 54, 56). Whatever may be thought of Bell's distinction between a Qur'ān-period and a Book-period (and in any case he sees the two as overlapping to some extent), it is important to note that the word *qur'ān* does not always mean the volume in our hands (apart from the fact that it had not been completed). It can mean a single passage as in 10.61 and 13.31, and perhaps elsewhere; or it can mean something larger, but not necessarily the whole Qur'ān, since in 15.87 it seems to exclude the *mathānī*. One thing that is clear, however, is that in his closing years at Medina Muḥammad had moved far beyond thinking that his function was to be 'only a warner' and now regarded it as including the production of 'the Book' which was to be the scripture of his community.

This discussion of the conception of the prophetic vocation has extended beyond the Meccan period, since it would have been unsatisfactory to cut it off precisely at the Hijra, even if, in the absence of exact dating, that had been practicable.

V

Muḥammad and the Meccan Pagans

The Qur'ān says hardly anything about events in Mecca during the years when Muḥammad was proclaiming the religion of Islam. There are virtually no factual details about the persons who accepted Islam, and only a modicum of general information about the opponents. Most of this last is about the verbal arguments between these and Muḥammad. The present chapter is not concerned with the theological aspects of Qur'ānic teaching but tries to bring together the material that is of a primarily historical character.

1 THE ROOTS OF OPPOSITION

By about the year 600 AD the Meccans, sometimes by unscrupulous practices, had gained a virtual monopoly of the trade between the Indian Ocean and the Mediterranean. Mecca had become a prosperous town, but this had brought a deep malaise into the lives of the inhabitants, and this malaise provided fertile ground for the religion proclaimed by Muḥammad to take root and flourish. In *Muhammad at Mecca* an analysis of the malaise was given which still after thirty years seems to be on the whole sound, and in the present context it will suffice to mention briefly some of the main points. The fundamental trouble was the change from a nomadic economy to a mercantile one, since for success in desert life it was necessary to maintain the solidarity of the kin-group, whereas commerce tended to encourage individualism. The outlook of most Meccans was still largely that of their nomadic ancestors of a generation or two back, but some of the values of nomadism were being eroded away, as, for example, when clan chiefs who were also wealthy merchants showed themselves unconcerned about the welfare of needy members of their clans. Commercial success had gone to the heads of the great merchants. Not merely had they become engrossed in the making of money, but they had also come to believe that by their economic power and entrepreneurial expertise they could control events over a wide area. Most of the inhabitants of Mecca probably shared in the town's prosperity, but the gap between the very rich and the not-quite-so-rich seems to have widened, and it was from the latter group that most of the early Muslims came (as we learn from the Sīra).

In *Muhammad at Mecca* the relevance of the Qur'ān to this situation was examined. It was assumed that, if one wants to understand why there was opposition to Muḥammad's message, one must look at the themes put forward in those early passages of the Qur'ān where there is no mention of opposition. Much the same results would be obtained if a slightly different view of Qur'ānic dating was adopted, such as that of Blachère. In these early passages five main themes may be distinguished. Firstly, God's power and goodness are asserted. He creates each individual human being, and controls the forces of nature on which human life is dependent; but, unlike the impersonal, perhaps even malevolent, Time in which the nomads believed, God seeks the welfare of humankind. Secondly, every one will appear before God on the Last Day as an individual to be judged according to his deeds and assigned to Paradise (the Garden) or Hell (the Fire). This was a sanction, appropriate to persons of individualistic outlook, which encouraged the observance of traditional practices. Thirdly, the human response to God's goodness was to show gratitude to him and to worship him. Fourthly, the practical aspect of gratitude to God should be a readiness to use one's wealth to help the needy and unfortunate. Fifthly, Muḥammad had the special vocation of warning people about the Last Judgement and the danger of eternal punishment; the other aspects of his vocation do not come into the earliest passages.

It is not immediately apparent why these themes should have raised up vigorous opposition against Muḥammad, but when the passages expressing the third and fourth themes are looked at, it will be found that they contain severe criticisms of the merchants. Something of this has already been mentioned in speaking of Meccan attitudes to wealth, but it is worth emphasizing again that there was this explicit critique in the earliest passages. The following, arranged in Blachère's order, criticize the use of wealth.

> Humankind to its Lord is indeed ungrateful,
> and itself is witness to that,
> and in love of wealth is extreme.
> Do they not know? When the graves are emptied,
> and what is in the breasts is manifest,
> on that day their Lord will of them be well informed. (100.6–11)

> As for him who gives and is pious
> and believes in the best,
> we will ease his way to ease.
> As for him who is mean and wealth-proud
> and disbelieves the best,
> we will ease his way to hardship;
> his wealth avails him not when he perishes. (92.5–11)

> (The man condemned)
> believed not in God Almighty,

nor urged the feeding of the destitute,
so today he has no friend. (69.33–5)

Did you (Muḥammad) see him who turns away,
gives little and is mean?
Has he knowledge of the unseen, so as to see?
(This includes the certainty of punishment.) (53.33–5)

(Hell-fire) summons him who backed and turned away
and gathered and hoarded (wealth). (70.17f.)

Woe to every maligner, traducer,
who gathers wealth and tells it over,
thinking his wealth will make him immortal. (104.1–3)

No, indeed, you honour not the orphan,
nor urge the feeding of the destitute;
you devour the inheritance greedily
and love wealth ardently. (89.17–20)

Of the believers it is said contrariwise (51.19):

In their wealth was due share for the beggar and the outcast.

In Sūra 93.9f. Muḥammad himself, after being reminded of God's goodness to him, is told: 'so oppress not the orphan, repulse not the beggar'.

Besides these criticisms of the use of their wealth by the rich Meccans there were also some criticisms of their attitudes. One of the words used to describe these is *istaghnā*, which was mentioned in the earlier section on wealth (p.43) as combining the ideas of being wealthy and being independent of others, and 'wealth-proud' was suggested as a translation. The verse (92.8) just quoted, however, shows that this pride in wealth does not lead to ostentation, but rather to the man's being mean and ungenerous with his money and goods. A second word *ṭaghā* is linked with *istaghnā* in 96.6-8 (p.42), where it is stated that the attitude described by *ṭaghā* is due to seeing oneself *istaghnā*, that is, wealthy and independent, while failing to take into account the return to God for judgement. The primary meaning of *ṭaghā* appears to be to transgress or go beyond normal limits or to go to excess, and it is particularly used of a stream or torrent rising well above its usual height; in 69.11 it is used of the sea rising. Metaphorically it may suggest arrogance, insolence and presumption, but when it is used of the wealthy Meccans and similar people it seems to have the more precise meaning of being unduly confident about one's own power and importance. This would accord with the fact that it is several times applied to Pharaoh (90.11; 79.17; 20.24,43,45). It also gives a reasonable meaning for 52.32, where it is asked in respect of the pagan Meccans: 'Do their *aḥlām* bid them act thus, or are they a people *ṭāghūn*?' The word *aḥlām* here is the plural of *ḥilm*, which was traditionally the distinctive characteristic of the Meccans, their prudence or calculating caution in business matters (cf. p.43); and here it becomes ineffective not through hotheadedness but through excessive self-confidence and self-importance. In the parable of the ruined garden (68.17–33) the owners confess in the end that they were *ṭāghūn* (v.31), and by this seem to mean that they were so confident in their own powers that they overlooked their dependence on God. It is because this self-confident attitude leads to disregard for God and exclusive concern with this-worldly matters that it brings people to Hell:

> As for him who was self-confident
> and chose the nearer life,
> Hell, indeed, is the dwelling. (79.37–9)

These various criticisms of the Meccan merchants would by themselves justify a measure of opposition among them to Muḥammad and his nascent religious movement. Apart from this, however, the more far-sighted leaders must have realized that Muḥammad was a potential threat to their political power. Though he insisted that he was 'only a warner', his claim to be a prophet implied that he had a certain wisdom, and Arabs in general tended to think the wise man best fitted to direct the affairs of a community. Besides, as Muḥammad gained an increasing number of followers among people of moderate influence in Mecca, it would have been difficult for the leaders to go against any ruling he put forward; and he might conceivably bring a revelation forbidding some of their trading practices. A revelation prohibiting *ribā*, usually translated 'usury', did in fact come after the Hijra (2.275f.; etc.); but what exactly was prohibited originally is far from clear, and the prohibition seems to have been directed mainly against the Jews, and certainly was not felt to be disadvantageous to the commerce now being vigorously engaged in by Meccans converted to Islam.[1] The words in 88.21f., 'You are only a warner (*mudhakkir*), not a controller (or overseer—*muṣayṭir*) over them', imply that some Meccans thought there was a political threat from Muḥammad, even though he himself at that time believed that he had no political ambitions. There may also have been Meccans who supposed that by his criticisms Muḥammad was hoping to gain some financial advantage for himself, perhaps to obtain a greater share in the most lucrative trade. Something like this seems to be indicated by the fact that in many passages Muḥammad and other prophets are made to insist that they ask of their hearers no reward (*ajr*) for their preaching.[2]

From the Sīra we further learn that, as the merchants became aware that the Qur'ān was criticizing them, they made several attempts to persuade Muḥammad to stop his criticisms. He was to be offered both better commercial openings and marriage into one of the best families. These attempts are presumably what is referred to in the following passages:

> They almost seduced you from what we revealed to you,
> so that you invented against us something other;
> then they would have taken you as friend (*khalīl*).
> Had we not established you,
> you had almost inclined to them some little. (17.73f.)

> Obey not those who count (the message) lies;
> they would like if you would speak fairly,
> and (then) they would speak fairly. (68.8f.)

'Speaking fairly' probably means refraining from criticisms, though it might conceivably mean permitting the intercession of the pagan deities, regarded as angels (as in the story of the 'satanic verses'). That deities were involved is suggested by 39.64:

> Say (Muḥammad): Another than God do you bid me worship?

68.10–15 may be taken as describing the unpleasant persons with whom Muḥammad had to deal:

> Neither obey every hateful oath-monger,
> fault-finding, spreading slander,
> withholding the good, transgressing,
> greedy, interfering,
> because he has wealth and sons.
> When our signs are recited to him,
> he says, Old-world tales.

These thoughts lead on to the next section which describes how for a time Muḥammad became involved in something not unlike a compromise.

2 THE FINAL BREAK WITH PAGANISM

Although Muḥammad successfully resisted nearly all the blandishments and threats of his opponents, there was one point at which he came near to yielding to them. This may be referred to in some of the verses just quoted, but the clearest statement is in 22.52:

> Before you we sent neither messenger nor prophet
> but, when he desired,
> Satan threw (something) into his desire.
> Then God cancels what Satan throws in.

The meaning of the words translated 'desired' and 'desire' is disputed, but, even if 'recited' and 'recitation' are substituted, the story is hardly affected. This is given in several versions in the commentary of aṭ-Ṭabarī on 22.52. It is to the effect that, as Muḥammad was hoping to win over more of the Meccans by a conciliatory revelation, he began to receive the passage in Sūra 53 beginning:

Have you considered al-Lāt and al-'Uzzā
and Manāt the third, the other? (53.19f.)

At that point Satan intervened and 'threw' on Muḥammad's tongue the words:

These are the *gharānīq* exalted;
their intercession is to be hoped for;
such as they forget not.

(The third line is sometimes omitted, and may be interpreted 'are not forgotten'.) When Muḥammad spoke these words aloud in the hearing of the leading Meccans with whom he was sitting in the Ka'ba, they were overjoyed and prostrated themselves with him in an act of worship. Whatever the meaning of *gharānīq*—it is said to mean 'high-flying cranes'—the Meccans understood the verses as giving permission to appeal to these deities as intercessors. Later Muḥammad realized that these words had come from Satan and not from God, and received the true continuation of the revelation, as it is now found in the Qur'ān:

Are yours the male and his the female?
That were division unfair.
They are but names you and your fathers have named.
God sent down no warrant for them.
They follow only fancy and what they themselves want.
Yet guidance from their Lord has come to them. (53.21–3)

The effect of this Qur'ānic attack on the goddesses was the ending of the period of good relations between Muḥammad and the leading Meccans.

The first thing to be said about the story is that it cannot be a sheer invention. Muḥammad must at some point have recited as part of the Qur'ān the verses which were later rejected as satanic in origin. No Muslim could possibly have invented such a story about Muḥammad, and no reputable Muslim scholar would have accepted it from a non-Muslim unless fully convinced of its truth. The Muslims of today tend to reject the story since it contradicts their idealized picture of Muḥammad; but, on the other hand it could be taken as evidence that Muḥammad was 'a human being like themselves' (41.6; etc).[3]

The three goddesses were probably singled out because they had important shrines not far from Mecca, that of al-Lāt being in the town of aṭ-Ṭā'if; and the hearers would probably think primarily of worship at these shrines. On the other hand, one of the Meccan leaders, Abū Sufyān, is said to have taken images of al-Lāt and al-'Uzzā with him into the battle of Uḥud;[4] in 4.76 it is said that, in contrast to the believers who fight 'in the way of God', the unbelievers fight 'in the way of the *ṭāghūt* or idol'. As indicated above, the cult of the goddesses rested more on residual belief than on active faith. Female deities were often known as 'the daughters of God' (*banāt Allāh*), and this phrase explains the point made about sons and daughters in the true continuation of the verses.

The difficult but important question is how in the first place Muḥammad came to accept the verses as genuine. In general it is to be assumed that when he received a revelation he approved of it and accepted its teaching; but, if it contained some novel point, he would surely consider whether this was consonant with his own previous thinking on kindred matters. How then can we explain his readiness to accept verses which apparently recognized three goddesses and thus went against the strict monotheism which is characteristic of Islam? One part of the answer to this is to insist that the dubious verses did not recognize the three goddesses as goddesses but only as beings who could intercede; and, as has been seen, there are a number of verses in the Qur'ān which imply that the deities of the pagans are really a kind of angel. If Muḥammad believed that the three were angels, this would not be a breach with monotheism, since monotheism can accept a belief in angels as created beings.

It has further to be noted that in the early passages of the Qur'ān there is no assertion that *Allāh* is uniquely God. It is possible that Muḥammad himself to some extent shared the belief of many of his contemporaries that *Allāh* was a high god with whom other beings could intercede. It is unlikely that he thought of these beings as lesser deities, but, as just suggested, he may have thought of them as angels. It is a curious fact, which may have some relevance here, that in the earliest passages of the Qur'ān the name *Allāh* is rarely used. Of the first thirty sūras in Blachère's order it occurs only in ten (apart from the *basmala* or initial invocation); and in most of these the verses in which it occurs appear to be later than most of the sūra, some looking as if they might have been added at the end by the later 'collectors'. In contrast to this 'your Lord' (*rabbu-ka*) or 'Lord' with another pronoun occurs in over twenty sūras, and often several times in each. This suggests that at the heart of Muḥammad's religious experience were the two visions of 53.1–18, and that he thought of the being there seen as 'his Lord' rather than as *Allāh* as commonly conceived by the Meccans. The acknowledgement of *Allāh* by the polytheists may have made it difficult to think of him monotheistically. Gradually, however, Muḥammad must have come to see that 'the Lord' he had experienced was indeed *Allāh* as recognized by Jews, Christians and others, and was uniquely God. The attributes and functions of God are in fact ascribed to 'your Lord' in many of the early verses. It is impossible to know how far Muḥammad's thinking about these matters had progressed by the time the satanic verses came to him, but there is no reason to suppose that he regarded the beings alleged to intercede as more than angels.

In the Sīra the incident of the satanic verses has links with the migration of a number of Muslims to Abyssinia to escape persecution, but the details of the accounts do not inspire much confidence and may be neglected here, since there is no reference in the Qur'ān. Likewise the Sīra gives no clear indication of how long it was before Muḥammad discovered that the verses were satanic. The situation was such, however, that he must soon have discovered whether the Meccan leaders were prepared to continue sharing in worship with the Muslims, perhaps once a week. Even if they were prepared to join in worship, he must also soon have discovered whether their acceptance of the Qur'ān was going to lead to a change in their life-style, and in particular in their use of their money. It was doubtless when he realized that they were not going to change their life-style, that he saw that the verses would have to be reconsidered. He may all along have been unhappy about the acknowledgement of the deities even as angels. When it became clear that the current belief in *Allāh* as high god with whom other beings might intercede was closely associated with the attitudes and practices criticized in the Qur'ān, the need for a break with this type of belief must have suggested itself. It is not necessary to suppose that Muḥammad thought the matter out explicitly. The idea of a break may have come to him first by revelation, but when it came he would at once realize that it was the best course of action.

The cancellation of the satanic verses and their replacement by others did not constitute a break, but must have made one inevitable. Whether this happened all at once or came about by stages is impossible to tell. The completeness of the break is emphasized in Sūra 109:

> Say: O unbelievers, I worship not what you worship;
> you are not worshipping what I worship;
> I am not worshipping what you have worshipped;
> you are not worshipping what I worship.
> Your religion for you, my religion for me.

This does not indicate, however, the new emphases in Qur'ānic teaching. Three complementary themes may be distinguished: the pagan deities are shown to have no reality; the unicity of God is insisted on; the sin is denounced of 'giving partners to God' (*shirk*), that is, of associating other beings with him as sharers in his divinity. All this seems to be directed mainly against the belief in *Allāh* as a high god, but the first theme also counters any residual belief in the pagan deities as war-gods which is suggested by the phrase about the unbelievers fighting 'in the way of the *ṭāghūt* or idol' (4.76) and Abū-Sufyān's taking images into battle.

The attack on the pagan deities does not begin with an outright denial of their existence but rather emphasizes their powerlessness. In 10.34f. the unbelievers are asked whether any of their 'partner-gods' (*shurakā'*) can create, restore to life and guide, as God does; and the implication is that they cannot. In 29.17 Abraham tells his people that those they worship other than God are unable to give them any provision (*rizq*). Of greater moment is the conception of 'help' (*naṣr*) in the special sense of protection by force if necessary (cf. p.20); the unbelievers are said to have hoped for 'help' from those they took as deities apart from God, but the latter are unable to 'help' them (36.74f.). The point is made more fully in 7.194–7:

> Those you call on apart from God are (his) servants like you;
> so call upon them and let them answer you, if you speak truth.
> Have they feet to walk with, or hands to hold with,
> or eyes to see with, or ears to hear with?
> Call upon your partner-gods;
> then plot against me, sparing me not.
> My protector (*walī*) is God, who sent down the Book;
> he protects the upright.

In 10.18 it is stated that those the unbelievers worship other than God can neither harm them nor benefit them, though they call them intercessors (*shufa'ā'*). In 39.43 those they take as intercessors are powerless and mindless, while intercession is entirely for God to decide.

There are a number of references to the relation of the unbelievers to their deities on the Last Day. In one verse (21.98) both the unbelievers and what they worship are said to be 'fuel of Hell'. Elsewhere the beings worshipped are accepted as innocent, but do nothing for the worshippers. In 28.63f. the worshipped admit leading the worshippers astray, but protest to God they are innocent, apparently on the grounds that they did not accept the worship; then the unbelievers are told to call on their partner-gods, but the latter give no answer. Somewhat similar is 25.17f.:

> On the day he assembles them and what they worship apart from God
> he says, Did you lead my servants astray,
> or did they stray from the (true) way?

They will say, Glory to you! we had no need
to take apart from you protectors (*awliyā'*);
but you gave them and their fathers a good life
until they forgot the warning and became a people worthless.

Other passages are:

When those who gave partners to God see their partner-gods,
they will say, O Lord, these are our partner-gods
whom we called upon apart from you;
but (these) will throw at them the words, You are lying. (16.86)

On the day we assemble them all,
then say to those who gave partners,
To your place, you and your partner-gods!
and make separation between them;
and their partner-gods will say, Not us were you serving;
God suffices as witness between us and you,
that of your worship we were unaware. (10.28f.)

In all these passages and in a number of briefer references there is no attempt to deny the existence of the beings worshipped, but they are described as powerless to do anything for the worshippers and as repudiating them. The term *shurakā'* has been translated 'partner-gods' although it is literally only 'partners' and thus says nothing about what these beings are in themselves apart from the false allegations of the worshippers. There seems to be a suggestion in the word, however, that they are junior partners, not equals. In 21.99 the fact that they are destined for Hell is said to show that they are not gods. Elsewhere, however, as has already been mentioned several times, they are sometimes regarded as angels. One passage where the identification of the deities with angels is implied is 43.19f.:

They make the angels, who are servants of the Merciful, females.
Did they witness their creation?
Their witness will be recorded,
and they will be questioned.
They said, Had the Merciful willed,
we had not worshipped them . . .

There are also traces of an identification of the deities with jinn, but it is not clear whether the worshippers made this identification or whether it is made first by the Qur'ān.

One day he will assemble them all,
then say to the angels, Were these worshipping you?
They say, Glory to you! you are our protector against them;

they are worshipping the jinn;
most of them believe in them. (34.40f.)

They ascribe to God as partner-gods the jinn,
though them he created; and in ignorance
they impute to him sons and daughters . . . (6.100)

One day we said to the angels, Bow down to Adam;
and they bowed down except Iblīs, who was of the jinn
and went against the command of his Lord.
Take you him and his offspring as protectors against me?
A bad exchange for the wrongdoers! (18.50)

While the negative points about the pagan deities are made clearly, there is obviously no single line of positive teaching about them, whether they are angels or jinn or nothing at all. The most extreme statement about them occurs in the passage replacing the satanic verses (though probably as a later addition):

These are but names you and your fathers have named.
God sent down no warrant for them. (53.23)

The same words are used by the prophet Hūd in arguing with his people (7.71) and by Joseph in arguing with his fellow-prisoners (12.40). They seem to mean that there is no reality corresponding to the names, and this is what one might expect the final Qur'ānic teaching to be. It is conceivable, however, that the words originally meant that the pagans gave the angels names which suggested that they were more than angels (al-Lāt, 'the goddess'; al-'Uzzā, 'the strong one'), and that for this they had no warrant. This interpretation is partly borne out by 53.27: 'those who believe not in the world-to-come name the angels with names of females'. On the other hand, the passages where the same words are used by Hūd and Joseph support the first interpretation. What is a little surprising is that this way of thinking does not seem to have replaced the arguments about powerlessness and the like where there was no denial of their existence. These last were perhaps more effective with the pagans with whom Muḥammad was in touch. It is also likely that the partner-gods were not a great problem in Medina, in contrast to Mecca, and that the matter received little attention after the Hijra.

Complementing these various assertions about the ungodlike character of the pagan deities is a second theme, the insistence on the sinfulness of invoking other deities or partnering other beings with God. This is implied in many of the passages already quoted, where the worshippers of these deities are depicted as about to be consigned to Hell. There are also explicit commands:

Make not along with God another deity;
I am a clear warner to you from him. (51.51)

Call not on another deity along with God,
and so become of the punished. (26.213)

Who calls on another deity along with God
has no proof thereof;
his reckoning is only with his Lord. (23.117)

In later Islam polytheism, or worshipping deities other than God, became the greatest sin, and was known as 'partnering' or 'associating' (*shirk*). This word only occurs once in this sense in the Qur'ān, in a passage where the ancient Arabian sage Luqmān exhorts his son: 'My son, do not partner (any being) with God; partnering (*shirk*) is great wrong'. Another passage, while emphasizing that *shirk* is the unforgivable sin, introduces some further curious ideas:

God pardons not partnering with him
though he pardons what is short of that to whom he will.
He who partners with God has strayed afar.
Apart from him they call only upon females,
and they call upon a Satan rebellious,
whom God cursed; he said, Of your servants
I will indeed take an appointed portion,
will lead them astray, will fill them with desires . . .
Who takes Satan as protector against God is a loser clear.
He promises them, fills them with desires,
but what he promises is only deception.
For these their abode is Hell;
they will find no refuge from it. (4.116–21)

The third theme is insistence on the unicity of God. This theme decisively separated the Muslims from any believers in *Allāh* as high god. It came to be such a central characteristic of Islam that it became the first clause of the Shahāda or Confession of Faith: 'there is no deity but God'. One of the early passages relevant to the break with the pagans is Sūra 112:

Say: He is God, One,
God the Supreme;
he neither begat nor was begotten.
A peer to him was none.

Another early passage is:

Mention the name of your Lord
and devote yourself wholly to him,
Lord of the East and the West; there is no deity but he.
Take him as your warden. (73.8f.)

It is curious that in the precise wording of this basic credal assertion there again seems to be a tendency to avoid *Allāh*. The form used in the later Shahāda occurs twice in the Qur'ān (37.35; 47.19), but in contrast to this the form 'there is no deity but he' occurs nearly thirty times, though admittedly several of these are preceded by *Allāh*, namely: 'God, there is no deity but he'. Another curious fact which might just be connected with this apparent avoidance of *Allāh* is that there was a time when the name ar-Raḥmān 'the Merciful', seemed to be replacing *Allāh*. The name ar-Raḥmān occurs over fifty times in the Qur'ān (apart from the *basmala*), but of these occurrences over forty are in the sūras of Blachère's second Meccan period. Could this have been due to continuing difficulties resulting from the popular use of *Allāh* for the high god?

In some of the passages which include the words 'there is no deity but he' there is also mention of his powers and attributes. The fullest is:

> God it is who made the night for your rest
> and the day for seeing;
> God is bountiful to humankind,
> but most people are ungrateful.
> That is God, your Lord, creator of all things,
> there is no deity but he . . .
> God it is who made the earth for you a dwelling
> and the heaven a canopy,
> who formed you and formed you well,
> and gave you provision of good things.
> That is God, your Lord; blessed be God, Lord of the worlds.
> He is the Living; there is no deity but he.
> Call upon him as sole object of devotion.
> Praise is God's, Lord of the worlds. (40.61–5)

As was noted above (p.34), the phrase 'as sole object of devotion' (*mukhliṣīn la-hu d-dīn*) seems specially directed against belief in *Allāh* as high god. The phrase in 73.8 translated as 'devote yourself to him alone' is *tabattal ilay-hi tabtīlan,* and probably has a similar import.

The materials which have been brought together to illustrate this 'final break with paganism' seem to make it clear that it was a process rather than a single event. Altogether, however, it meant that from this time on Muḥammad would have to meet more determined opposition from the leading men of Mecca. The Sīra mentions various ways in which life was made difficult for Muḥammad and the Muslims, but before looking at the Qur'ānic evidence, a brief account may be given of the verbal attacks on Muḥammad and his religion.

3 VERBAL ARGUMENTS

To judge from what is said in the Qur'ān the verbal arguments of the opponents were directed mainly against two points: the teaching about the Last Judgement; and Muḥammad's claim to be a prophet and receive revelations from God. Though the wealthy Meccans must have resented the criticism of their use of their wealth, they were apparently not prepared to offer any public defence of their practices. The nearest to such a defence—if it may be applied to Mecca—is the complaint made to Shu'ayb by his people that the religion he preaches will stop them doing what they like with their wealth (11.87).

A *the Last Judgement*

The teaching about the Last Judgement was not, of course, unconnected with the criticism of the use of wealth, since, if one believed that the Judgement would take place, this would lead to a change in life-style. The connection between the unbelief of the merchants and their current practices is shown in 107.1–3:

> Have you seen him who counts false the Judgement?
> That is he who repulses the orphan,
> and urges not the feeding of the destitute.

A favourite point with the opponents seems to have been to deride the possibility of restoring dead bodies to life, since without a resurrection there can be no Judgement. They probably felt they had a strong point here.

> Before that they were in luxury
> and were continuing in the heinous sin,
> saying, When we die and are dust and bones,
> shall we be raised again?
> and also our fathers of old? (56.45–8)

The following passage has the beginnings of a reply:

> No, I swear by the day of resurrection,
> I swear by the self-blamer,
> does a person think we shall not bring together his bones?
> Truly, we are able to restore his fingers.
> Rather he wants to go forward sinning;
> he asks, When is the day of resurrection? (75.1–6)

The objection was in fact met in various ways. Some passages have already been quoted (p.8) in which the coming of rain to parched and 'dead' earth is seen as a sign of God's power to raise human beings from the dead. Another argument is that, since God has power to create a person in the first place, he has also power to restore him to life.

Has man not considered that we created him from a drop?
He is an opponent clear;
he coined for us a parable,
and forgot his being created.
He said, Who revives the bones when decayed?
Say: He revives them who first produced them;
of all creation he is knowing. (36.77–9)

Does man think he was left to himself?
Was he not a seed emitted?
then a blood-clot? Then he shaped and fashioned him,
and made him the pair, the male and the female.
Has that one not the power to raise the dead? (75.36–40)

There were also opponents who directly denied any Judgement.

Woe that day to those counting false,
who count false the Day of Judgement.
There count it false none but the guilty sinner,
who, when our signs are recited to him, says,
Old-world tales! (83.11–13)

Sometimes again it was Hell that was denied.

Woe on that day to those counting false,
whose discourse is frivolous;
the day they are rudely thrust into the fire of Hell,
This is the fire you were counting false;
is this magic, or are you not seeing (well)? (52.11–15)

Another line taken by the opponents was to ask Muḥammad when this disaster was to come upon them, implicitly suggesting that, since it was so long delayed, it might never happen.

They ask you about the Hour, when its coming is,
how you came to mention it.
To your Lord is its ending;
you are only the warner of him who fears it. (79.42–5)

They say, When will this promise be,
if you are speakers of truth? . . .
No, it will come upon them suddenly, astounding them;
they will be unable to avert it,
nor will they have respite. (21.38,40)

B *Muḥammad's prophethood*

The opponents were unable to deny the existence of the revelations Muḥammad had claimed to have received, but they cast doubts on the claim that they were from God. They probably also had to admit that there was something unusual about the revelations, since nothing like them existed in Arabic; and this uniqueness was emphasized by the Qur'ānic challenges to produce something similar, and their failure to do so.

A common line of attack was to describe Muḥammad as *majnūn*, the normal word for 'mad' but originally meaning 'possessed by jinn'.[5]

> How shall there be for (the unbelievers) the warning,
> seeing that there came to them a clear messenger?
> Then they turned from him and said,
> 'Taught (by other), *majnūn*'. (44.13f.)

Since the jinn were sometimes malevolent, there could be no certainty the messages they brought were true, and so all the teaching of the Qur'ān could be disregarded. Muḥammad seems to have been somewhat perturbed when the accusation of being possessed was first made against him.

> The unbelievers had almost made you stumble
> their looks when they heard the reminder,
> saying, He is *majnūn*. (68.51)

There are several passages addressed to Muḥammad himself, assuring him that he is not *majnūn*.

> Warn, you by the grace of your Lord
> are neither soothsayer nor *majnūn*. (59.29; cf. 68.2; 81.22)

Various other similar terms were also applied to him, such as 'soothsayer' (*kāhin*), in 52.29 and 69.42, 'poet' (*shā'ir*) in 69.41, and 'magician' (*sāḥir*) in 38.4. These words all suggest that Muḥammad was under the influence of supernatural powers of some sort. Poets at this time were supposed to have a familiar spirit or *jinnī* (genie), and the Qur'ān uses the phrase *shā'ir majnūn* (37.36). On the other hand, poetry was the one highly developed branch of Arabic literature, and it should have been obvious that the rhythmic and assonanced prose (*saj'*) of the early passages was distinct from poetry. The statement in 36.69 that God 'did not teach him the (art of) poetry (*shi'r*)' can hardly be questioned. The Qur'ān bluntly denies all such charges made against Muḥammad.

Another line of attack was to allege that Muḥammad had human collaborators, or that he himself had invented the Qur'ān. The alleged human collaborators are mentioned in 16.103 and 25.4f., which were discussed above (p.45); their existence was not directly denied, but in 16.103 it was argued that, since the person referred to was a foreigner, he could not have produced good Arabic. The charge that Muḥammad himself had 'invented' or 'forged' the Qur'ān (*iftarā-hu*; 32.3; etc.), that is, had himself thought it out and composed it, is rebutted by speaking of the dire punishments that would be inflicted on him if he dared to do anything of this kind (see p.69.). The following passage brings together the charges of being a magician and of inventing the revelation, and shows that denial of the pagan deities was a part of what he was accused of inventing.

> They wondered that a warner, one of them, has come to them,
> and the unbelievers said, This is a lying magician.
> Makes he the deities one God?
> That is something amazing.
> The leaders of them go apart (saying),
> Be off, and hold fast to your deities.
> This is a thing wanted.
> We heard not of this in the later religion;
> this is only an invention (*ikhtilāq*). (38.4–7)

Lastly various points are made involving Muḥammad's humanity. Some opponents thought that messages of such importance as the Qur'ān claimed to be should have been entrusted to someone of greater dignity than Muḥammad—for example, 'to a great one of the two towns' (43.31), or even to an angel.

> They said, Why was not an angel sent down to him?
> Had we sent down an angel, the matter had been decided,
> and they would have had no postponement.
> Had we made him (the messenger) an angel,
> we had made him a man (in form),
> and had confused for them what they are now confusing. (6.8f.)

Alternatively it was thought that the claim to prophethood should be accompanied by signs. Mostly only signs in general are spoken of, but one passage gives examples:

> They said, We will not believe in you,
> until you produce from the earth for us a spring;
> or have a garden of date-palms and vines
> and in it cause rivers to gush forth;
> or bring down the heaven on us in fragments, as you said;
> or come with God and the angels before (us);
> or have an ornamented house,
> or ascend into heaven;
> and we shall not believe in your ascent
> until you bring down to us a book to recite.
> Say: Glory be to my Lord!
> Am I aught but a human messenger? (17.90–3)

In response to such demands Muḥammad is to say that he is 'only a human being like you, to whom it has been revealed that your god is one God' (41.6; cf. 18.110). He has no special knowledge of divine matters or of the future.

> Say: I say not to you
> that 'I have the treasuries of God'
> nor that 'I know the unseen'.
> I say not to you, 'I am an angel'.
> I only follow what is revealed to me . . . (6.50)

It was presumably other opponents who argued that the Qur'ānic messages were not to be believed because they were a purely human production. Their unique character is admitted by speaking of them as 'magic' (*siḥr*), but this is then taken to be a human trick and nothing more, though perhaps one 'handed down' by a tradition.

> Had we sent down to you (Muḥammad) a book on parchment
> for them to touch with their hands,
> the unbelievers would have said,
> This is only magic clear. (6.7)

> (An unbeliever) said, This is only magic handed down;
> this is only the speech of a human being. (74.24f.)

> The wrongdoers said, This is only a human being like you;
> do you accept the magic, seeing it (to be such)? (21.3)

Altogether there was little consistency in the arguments of Muḥammad's opponents against him.

C *the stories of former prophets*

An important part of the Qur'ānic defence of Muḥammad's position against his opponents consists in references to the experiences of earlier prophets. This has several distinct functions.

The Arabs in general, and especially the nomads, abhorred novelty, and one of the criticisms made against Muḥammad was that this bringing of revelations purporting to be from God was something new, an aspect of religion that had been unknown to 'the fathers' (see 23.24; etc.). Besides insisting that Muḥammad was not a *bid'*, something new or a novelty (46.9), the Qur'ān amply illustrated the point by its numerous references to previous prophets or messengers. These constituted, as it were, Muḥammad's spiritual ancestry. His message was, in essentials, the same as theirs and confirmed what had been revealed to them.

Several of the references to prophets emphasize that, when God sent one to a people and they rejected his message, God punished this people by some natural disaster, such as the flood which destroyed 'the people of Noah'. In some of the earliest passages (such as 53.50–4 and 89.6–14) there is no mention of a messenger but only of the people or tribe and their punishment, and the punishment is said to be for their wickedness. The examples given are the ancient Arabian tribes of 'Ād and Thamūd, Pharaoh and his people, Noah's people and the 'overwhelmed towns' (probably Sodom and Gomorrah). In 69.4–10 the reason for punishment is given as disbelief in the Last Judgement; a messenger is spoken of in verse 10, though not named, but this verse looks like a later addition. In most of the later versions of these stories, however, the emphasis changes, and the fault of those punished consists in rejecting the message that has come to them and disobeying the messenger. An example of this is in Sūra 26 where there are passages about Noah (vv.105–22), 'Ād and the prophet Hūd (123–40), Thamūd and the prophet Ṣāliḥ (141–59), Lot and his people (160–75), and Shu'ayb and his people (176–91). Several sūras have similar collections of 'punishment stories'.[6]

The point of these stories varies in different sūras. Sometimes it is the severity of the punishment of the unbelievers that is emphasized, but in other versions it may be the fact that God protects and delivers the prophet and the believers. Indeed one of the purposes of the stories is to encourage the believers to remain faithful to Islam even when life is difficult. For this the stories of Noah and Lot are more appropriate than some of the others.

When a collection of such stories is placed together in a sūra, they tend (as in Sūra 26) to be given a similar form, and many verses may be repeated almost word for word. Such repetitions raise the suspicion that many of the details in these stories are not derived from historical tradition but merely reflect the experiences of Muḥammad and the Muslims in Mecca. Distinctive features are, of course, retained; the people of Noah are drowned by the flood, while he is saved by the ship; 'Ād are destroyed by an exceptionally strong wind, Thamūd by an earthquake or a 'shout'. The following passage would appear to be closer to the experience of Muḥammad than that of Noah:

> Noah we sent to his people; he said,
> O my people, worship God; you have no deity but him;
> will you not be (god)fearing?
> The leaders of his people, unbelievers, said,
> This is only a human being like you
> who wants to have superiority over you;
> had God willed, he would have sent down angels;
> we heard not of this among our fathers formerly.

He is only a man possessed;
so watch him for a time (to see what happens).
(Noah) said, O my Lord, help me,
since they count me false.
We 'indicated' to him, Make the boat
under our eyes and by our indication. (23.23–7)

In so far as this reflects conditions in Mecca, it shows that Muḥammad was suspected of wanting power and was felt to be making a break with ancestral tradition. Similar points appear in an account of Moses and Aaron. Pharaoh's courtiers say to them:

Have you come to turn us
from (the religion) we found our fathers following,
so that greatness in the land may be yours? (10.78)

In the passage about an unnamed prophet following the one about Noah just quoted there occur the words:

The leaders of his people, unbelievers
denying the meeting of the Hereafter,
whom we had enriched in this nearer life, said,
This is only a human being like you,
eating what you eat and drinking what you drink.
If you obey a human being like yourselves,
you then are the losers. (23.33f.)

In this way charges made against Muḥammad are repeated in the case of other prophets. Good points are also mentioned. When Ṣāliḥ summoned his people to worship God, they rejected his appeal, but in doing so expressed disappointment; they had set high hopes on him (11.62) and he had let them down. Somewhat similarly the prophet Shu'ayb is described as one who had previously been 'prudent' (*ḥalīm*) and 'of sound judgement' (*rashīd*) (11.87). If these terms can be applied to Muḥammad, that would confirm some of the things said in the Sīra about his reputation among the Meccans before his call to prophethood. In the stories of the prophets there are so many little details of this kind which fit in perfectly with what we know about Muḥammad and life in Mecca, that it is difficult to avoid the conclusion that they are indeed reflections of Meccan conditions. On the other hand, it would be rash to suppose that every detail is necessarily something which existed or happened in Mecca.

4 PERSECUTION AND THE HIJRA

In the Sīra-material there are a number of stories about the persecution of Muḥammad and his followers by their opponents, and some sort of persecution is implied by the description of the Emigrants at Medina as 'those who emigrated after they had been persecuted (*futinū*)' (16.110), and probably also by the assertion in 85.10 that 'those who persecuted (*fatanū*) believing men and women, and did not repent' are destined for Hell. Some of the acts spoken of in the Sīra are annoying and offensive but hardly amount to persecution, and so it is difficult to know just how much or how little is comprised in the word 'persecuted' in these verses. Even in the Qur'ān the verb *fatana* and the noun *fitna* have several meanings which vary from the infliction of suffering to attempts to seduce believers from the true faith.[7] Various other passages of the Qur'ān give some hints about what constituted hostile treatment of the Muslims.

One of the earliest hostile acts seems to have been preventing a Muslim from praying.

> Have you seen him who forbids
> a servant when he prays?
> Have you seen if he follows guidance
> or bids to piety?
> Have you seen if he counts false and turns away?
> Does he not know that God sees? . . .
> No, obey him not, but bow down and draw near. (96.9–14,19)

The word 'servant' (*'abd*) properly means 'slave', but it is commonly used in the Qur'ān for human beings as God's servants or slaves, and that is probably the meaning here rather than an actual slave; indeed the word is sometimes held by Muslims to refer here to Muḥammad himself. In 41.26 there seems to be a description of an attempt on the part of unbelievers to prevent the Qur'ān being recited by making irreverent noises during the recitation.

There are also hints that Muḥammad was deeply pained by some of the things said about him or to him. In 15.97 God knows 'that your breast is contracted by what they say'; while in 94.1–4 Muḥammad is reminded how God has helped him in such difficulties:

> Did we not expand your breast
> and take from you your burden,
> which weighed on your back,
> and enhance your reputation?

In the Sīra Muḥammad is taunted with being *abtar*, that is, tailless or having his tail docked—a way of saying that he has no son; and this taunt is thrown back at the one who made it in 108.3. (This sūra sounds like an early Meccan sūra, but the description of Muḥammad as having been given 'abundance' (*al-kawthar*) would be more appropriate at

Medina.) In 36.76 Muḥammad is told not to let himself be grieved by what they say, since God knows both what they keep secret and what they say publicly (cf. 27.70; 10.65).[8]

The Sīra shows that the most serious forms of persecution were those which occurred within the clan or family. Owing to the system of 'protection' on which life in Mecca was based (see pp. 17–20) a Muslim had little to fear from opponents outwith his own clan. Within the clan, however, various forms of physical constraint were possible. This is probably what is referred to in the following passage, describing an altercation on the Last Day:

> The unbelievers said, We will not believe in this Qur'ān
> nor in what was before it.
> But would you might see when the wrongdoers,
> stationed before their Lord, wrangle one with another,
> the weak saying to the proud,
> But for you we would be believers.
> The proud shall say to the weak, Did we bar you
> from the guidance after it came to you?
> No, you acted wrongly.
> And the weak shall say to the proud,
> No, (it was) your scheming night and day,
> when you bade us show ingratitude to God,
> and to set up rivals for him.
> They shall conceal their regret when they see the punishment
> and when we set chains on the unbelievers' necks.
> Is their recompense not solely for what they were doing?(34.31–3)

The 'proud' (*alladhīna stakbarū*) are the leaders of the clan or extended family, while the 'weak', more precisely 'those reckoned weak' (*alladhīna staḍʿafū*), were less influential members of the clan or family, such as sons and younger brothers. The 'weak' could, of course, also include those only attached to a clan and for that reason given only a bare minimum of 'protection'.

So long as Muḥammad's uncle Abū-Ṭālib was head of the clan of Hāshim, Muḥammad was fully protected. This situation is probably reflected in the passage in 11.91f. about Shuʿayb:

> They said, O Shuʿayb
> not much of what you say do we understand;
> and we see you weak (*ḍaʿīf*) among us;
> but for your *rahṭ* we had stoned you;
> with us you count not for much.
> He said, O my people, with you
> does my *rahṭ* count more than God?

Scholars have discussed whether *rahṭ* here means a kin-group or a group of mixed descent, such as the group of Muḥammad's leading followers like Abū-Bakr and 'Umar. It seems that it must have been a kin-group, since Muḥammad's followers were unable to 'protect' him in the last critical months at Mecca; but it is possible that this was a contemptuous way of referring to a kin-group—like calling them 'gang'—suggesting that they were weak. 'Count for much, more' has been used to translate *'azīz, a'azz*, which basically mean 'strong' or 'great' but here refer to importance or influence in the community.

We learn from the Sīra that after Abū-Ṭālib died Muḥammad, before returning to Mecca from a journey to aṭ-Ṭā'if, had to ask for 'protection' from the head of another clan, and was only granted it at his third request. This implies that the new head of his clan, Abū-Lahab, had refused him 'protection', at least on terms Muḥammad was prepared to accept. This is doubtless the reason for the bitter attack on Abū-Lahab in Sūra 111. It was traditionally during his return journey from aṭ-Ṭā'if, that a band of jinn came to Muḥammad, listened to his preaching and were converted (46.29–32; 72.1–19); jinn, like human beings, have been created to serve God (51.56).

There does not appear to be any explicit command to Muḥammad and the Muslims to leave Mecca, unless the words in 73.10 'withdraw from them gracefully' (where 'withdraw', *ahjur*, is the verb from which Hijra comes) can be taken as such a command. In some ways this would be an appropriate command, but unfortunately the likelihood is that the verse was revealed for some other occasion, perhaps for the time when most of the other clans were boycotting Hāshim. The Qur'ānic word for 'emigrate' is *hājara*, the third stem, which means a mutual cutting off from friendly or loving communion or intercourse. It does not appear to have been used in the Qur'ān, however, until after the emigration had taken place. The word *hijra* does not occur in the Qur'ān. It is just conceivable that the phrase 'the land of God is wide' (39.10; cf. 29.56) was intended to encourage the Muslims to emigrate, but the occasion could have been other than at the time of Muḥammad's own Hijra.

Nothing about the negotiations with Medina is to be learnt from the Qur'ān. The terms of the Pledge of the Women, which was made by a number of Muslims from Medina at the pilgrimage of 621, were held by Muslim scholars to be contained in 60.12, and in a sense this is correct; but the actual verse was not revealed until relatively late in the Medinan period. The same is true of verses held to permit the Muslims to fight.[9] That which says, 'Fight them until there is no persecution (*fitna*) and the religion is God's alone' (8.39), was probably not revealed until after the battle of Badr. More appropriate is 22.39f.:

Permission is given to those who fight because wronged—
God is indeed able to 'help' them—
who were driven out from their homes unjustly . . .

This is possibly the earliest verse about fighting, but it can hardly have been revealed at Mecca, since the Muslims have already been expelled. While still at Mecca Muḥammad must have foreseen that he would probably be involved in fighting with the pagan Meccans after he went to Medina, but the Qur'ān provides no evidence of a command about fighting being revealed at Mecca. Most of the verses about fighting clearly come in the later years at Medina.

It is presumably to the last year or two at Mecca that several verses about 'scheming' (*kayd*) and 'plotting' (*makr*) belong. Some of these verses are fairly general. Thus 86.15f. speaks of the unbelievers 'devising a scheme' (*yakīdūna kayd*), doubtless against Muḥammad, while God is also devising a scheme. Other verses emphasize God's knowledge of the schemes and plots (13.42; 14.46), even when they are arranged in complete secrecy (43.80). The aims of the opponents are stated in 8.30:

The unbelievers are plotting to stop you (Muḥammad)
or kill you or drive you out.
They were plotting and God was plotting,
but God is the best of plotters.

Some of the verses about other prophets may also be relevant here. A plot against Ṣāliḥ is described in 27.48–51, and one wonders how much of the detail reflects something that happened to Muḥammad.

There were in the city nine in a gang (*rahṭ*),
working evil in the land and not good.
They said, Swear to one another by God,
we will fall upon him and his household by night,
then we will say to the 'protector' (*walī*),
We witnessed not the destruction of his household,
speaking truthfully.
They plotted a plot and we plotted a plot
without their perceiving.
See the outcome of their plot;
we annihilated them and their people altogether.

Again in 28.20 Moses received warning of a plot:

A man came running from the outer town and said,
O Moses, the leaders take counsel against you to kill you;
so go away; I advise you well.

This suggests that some person may have warned Muḥammad about the Meccan leaders' plots, but this cannot be definitely asserted. In the Sīra it is said that the foiling of a plot against Muḥammad is referred to in 36.8f., where God is said to have placed a barrier before and behind some unbelievers and prevented them from seeing; and there may be some truth in this. Muḥammad was almost certainly aware that some opponents had designs on his life; and it seems likely that 21.34f. was intended to strengthen him when he felt thus threatened:

> Immortality we appointed for no human being before you;
> if you die, are they immortal?
> Every person is tasting death.
> We try you with evil and good as a test (*fitna*),
> and to us are you made to return.

The Qur'ān speaks of the Meccans as having driven out or expelled Muḥammad and the Muslims, using the word *akhraja*; and this suggests that the latter had little choice. Thus it is stated that God has destroyed towns stronger than Muḥammad's town which 'drove him out' (47.13). The Muslims are told not to take as 'friends' unbelievers, since these drove out both Muḥammad and themselves (60.1,9). A mysterious verse (17.76) speaks of the opponents 'almost scaring Muḥammad' so as to drive him out; and it has been suggested that this refers to some earlier occasion when he might have been expelled without taking his followers with him.[10] In 14.13 unbelievers say to unnamed messengers, 'We shall drive you out from our land unless you return to our creed'; and Shu'ayb is similarly addressed in 7.88; but this could hardly have applied to Muḥammad except at the early period when he was being asked to acknowledge the pagan deities, and at that time there was no question of expulsion, so far as we know. References to Lot being expelled because he set himself up as morally superior (7.82; 27.56) hardly seem to apply to Muḥammad just before the Hijra, and are aspects of the story of Lot.

Where the Sīra seems to be saying that it was of his own free will that Muḥammad decided to make the Hijra, the word 'driven out' (*akhraja*) implies that it was rather a matter of compulsion. Perhaps the element of constraint came from the fact that when Muḥammad was given 'protection' by another clan leader after his return from aṭ-Ṭā'if, it was on condition that he abandoned all attempts to propagate his religion, perhaps even gave up praying in public. The Sīra glosses over this point, perhaps because it was felt to be rather disgraceful for the clan of Hāshim; but the use of 'driven out' implies that Muḥammad and the Muslims felt that they were being forced to go, and the Qur'ān says nothing of possible advantages of going to Medina.

After some seventy Muslims had made their way to Medina in the year 622, Muḥammad set out with Abū-Bakr, following a devious route, since he could probably have been killed with impunity after leaving Mecca and before reaching the 'protection' of Medina. This is commemorated in 9.40:

> If you do not give him support, yet God supported him,
> when the unbelievers drove him out, the second of two;
> the two were in the cave, and he was saying to his companion,
> Do not grieve, God is with us.
> Then God sent down his *sakīna* upon him,
> and strengthened him with hosts you saw not;
> (thus) he made the word of the unbelievers lowest,
> while the word of God is highest.
> God is mighty, wise.

There is an Arabic word *sakīna*. 'tranquillity', but in the Qur'ān it is thought to have been influenced by the Hebrew *shechīnā* and to indicate the indwelling of God or a sense of his presence.[12] The translation 'assurance' might suit here.

Muḥammad and Abū-Bakr reached Medina safely on 24 September 622. The Meccan prophet was thus transformed into the prophet-statesman of Medina.

Bibliography of Works Referred to in the Text

Andrae, Tor *Mohammed the Man and his Faith* 2nd edition New York 1955

Bell, Richard *Introduction to the Qur'ān* Edinburgh 1953 (for revised edition see Watt)

The Qur'ān: translated with a critical rearrangement of the Surahs two vols Edinburgh 1937, 1939

Blachère, Régis *LeCoran: traduction selon un essai de reclassement des sourates* 1st edition, three vols Paris 1947, 1949, 1951

EI[1], *EI*[2] *Encyclopaedia of Islam* 1st, 2nd editions

Ibn Hishām *Sīra* ed F. Wüstenfeld Göttingen 1858-60

Jeffery, Arthur *The Foreign Vocabulary of the Qur'ān* Baroda 1938

Lane, E. W. *An Arabic-English Lexicon* London 1863-93

Nöldeke, Theodor *Geschichte des Qorāns* 1st edition 1860, 2nd edition revised by Fr. Schwally and others, three vols 1909, 1919, 1938, reprinted Hildesheim 1961

Paret, Rudi *Der Koran, Übersetzung* Stuttgart 1963-66

Der Koran, Kommentar und Konkordanz Stuttgart 1971

Trimingham, J. Spencer *Christianity among the Arabs in pre-Islamic Times* London 1979

Watt, W. Montgomery *Bell's Introduction to the Qur'ān* revised edition Edinburgh 1970

The Formative Period of Islamic Thought Edinburgh 1973

Muhammad at Mecca Oxford 1953

Muhammad at Medina Oxford 1956

Yāqūt *Mu'jam al-Buldān* ed F. Wüstenfeld Leipzig 1866-73

(bibliographical details of other works are given in the notes)

Notes

CHAPTER I

1 Watt, 'The Reliability of Ibn Isḥāq's Sources' in *La Vie du prophète Mahomet* (Colloque de Strasbourg, Oct. 1980), 31-43; an earlier version is 'The Materials used by Ibn Isḥāq' in B. Lewis and P. Holt (eds), *Historians of the Middle East*, London 1962.

2 Al-Bayḍāwī on 2.22; other verses are: 13.3; 51.48; 71.89; 78.6; 88.20.

3 5.116; 9.30.

4 See Bibliography.

5 See his Introduction and his translation.

6 See Bibliography.

CHAPTER II

1 The passages are arranged in Blachère's order, but there is no indication of change or development.

2 See al-Bayḍāwī's comment on 2.22.

3 Some commentators claim that the word *ibl* should be interpreted as 'clouds' here.

4 See Philip K. Hitti, *History of the Arabs*, fifth edn., London 1951, 54, 64f.

5 See *EI*², arts. Aṣḥāb al-Ukhdūd (Paret) and Dhū Nuwās (Al-Assouad). The argument against the older interpretation is best stated in Josef Horovitz, *Koranische Untersuchungen*, Berlin 1926, 12, 92f., and the view is also held by Hubert Grimme, Richard Bell and Rudi Paret.

6 *The Martyrs of Najrān: New Documents*, 1971, 46f. See also: Watt, 'The Men of the Ukhdūd (Sura 85)' in *The Muslim East: Studies in Honour of Julius Germanus*, ed. Gy. Kaldy-Nagy, Budapest 1974, 31-4.

7 Other similar verses are: 40.21, 82; 47.10; 12.109; 3.137; 16.36; 27.69; 30.42.

8 Watt, *Muhammad at Medina*, 372-92.

9 *EI*², art. 'Abd (R. Brunschvig); Robert Roberts, *The Social Laws of the Qorān*, London 1925 (1971), 53-60; Sura 4.92.

10 See al-Bayḍāwī's comment on 49.13.

11 See Jeffery, *Foreign Vocabulary*, s.v.

12 *Deuteronomy* 19.21; cf. *Exodus* 21.23f.; *Leviticus* 24.20.

13 See further *Muhammad at Medina*, 238-47.

14 Ibn Hishām, 727f.; *Muhammad at Medina*, 185-7.

15 See: 4.100; 22.58; 29.26.

16 See the remarks about Manāt in the next sub-section.

17 See Watt, *Formative Period*, 91.

18 *Psalm* 139.16, Jerusalem Bible.

19 51.58.

20 5.114; 22.58; 23.72; 34.39; 62.11.

21 24f.; see also Trimingham, *Christianity among the Arabs*, 243-8.

22 See: Julius Wellhausen, *Reste arabischen Heidentums*, second edn., Berlin 1897, reprinted 1927; Toufic Fahd, *Le Panthéon de l'Arabie centrale à la veille de l'hégire*, Paris 1968.

23 Helmer Ringgren, *Studies in Arabian Fatalism*, Uppsala 1955, 29, 41; cf. Fahd, op. cit., 123-6.

24 Ibn Hishām, 582.

25 Frants Buhl, *Das Leben Muhammeds*, tr. H. H. Schaeder, Leipzig 1930, 75, without references.

26 16.57; 17.40; 37.149,153; 43.15; 52.39; 53.21f.

27 Ringgren, *Studies*, 40f., 63f., 76, 79; in Muslim poets—143, 173.

28 In addition to 17.40 and 37.150 see 43.19 and 53.27.

29 See: Watt, 'Belief in a "high god" in pre-Islamic Mecca', *Journal of Semitic Studies*, xvi (1971), 35-40; also 'The Qur'ān and Belief in a "high god"', *Proceedings of the Ninth Congress of the Union Européenne des Arabisants et Islamisants*, Leiden 1981, 327-33. The first also appeared in the *Actes* of the Fifth Congress of the U.E.A.I. (Brussels 1970), 499-505, and the *Proceedings of the Twelfth Congress* (Stockholm 1970)... *for the History of Religion* (Leiden 1975), 228-34; and the second also in *Der Islam*, lvi (1979), 205-11.

30 Javier Teixidor, *The Pagan God: Popular Religion in the Greco-Roman Near East*, Princeton 1977, 17.

31 Ibid., 161f.

32 See: Trimingham, *Christianity among the Arabs*.

33 Arthur Jeffery, *Materials for the History of the Text of the Qur'ān*, Leiden 1937, 32 (from Ibn Mas'ūd).

34 Watt, 'Two Interesting Christian-Arabic Usages', *Journal of Semitic Studies*, ii (1957), 360-5.

35 See: aṭ-Ṭabarī, *History*, Leiden edition, i.1076. For what follows see the art. Ilāf in *EI*², which gives prominence to a hypothesis by M. Hamidullah for which the evidence is slender.

36 See: W. W. Barthold, 'Der Koran und das Meer', *Zeitschrift der deutschen morgenländischen Gesellschaft*, 83 (1929), 37-43; also *EI*¹, art. Fulk (H. Banes).

37 The word *yujbā* is used of collecting taxes, but it often means 'collect' in a general sense.

38 *The Commercial-Theological Terms in the Koran*, Leiden 1892. Tor Andrae, *Mohammed*, 86, suggests that the theological terms are borrowed from Syrian Christianity; but even if some conceptions came from this source, the appropriateness to the thinking of the Meccan merchants was also an important factor.

39 Bell, *Introduction*, 79; Watt, *Bell's Introduction*, 4.

CHAPTER III

1 Tor Andrae, *Mohammed*, 39.

2 Yāqūt, *Mu'jam al-Buldān*, iii.665.

3 Jeffery, *Foreign Vocabulary*, s.v. *ṣuḥuf*.

4 For *ummī* see Horovitz, *Koranische Untersuchungen*, Berlin 1926, 52f.; also *EI* (Shorter), art. *ummī* (R. Paret).

CHAPTER IV

1 Ibn Hishām, 150, 166.

2 Aṭ-Ṭabarī, *History*, i.1139-41.

3 Nöldeke-Schwally, *Geschichte des Qurāns*, second edn., i.21, n.2.

4 Karl Ahrens, *Muhammed als Religionsstifter*, Leipzig 1935, 133f. See also: Paret, *Kommentar*, on 2.109.

5 *Murūj adh-dhahab*, ed. C. Barbier de Meynard et al., Paris, 1861, etc., i.54.

6 The interpretation is discussed in *Muhammad at Medina*, 312f.

7 See his translation of the Qur'ān; also Watt, *Bell's Introduction*, 86-101.

8 For the interpretation see article referred to in ch.2, n.34.

9 Lane, *Lexicon*, s.v.; cf. Paret, *Kommentar*, 117f. (on 5.13).

10 Jeffery, *Foreign Vocabulary*, s.v.

11 Watt, *Bell's Introduction*, ch.8: original edition, ch.7.

CHAPTER V

1 *Muhammad at Medina*, but see Maxime Rodinson, *Islam and Capitalism*, London 1968, 239f., 250.

2 Muḥammad—6.90; 12.104; 25.57; 34.47; 38.56; 42.23; 52.40; 68.46. Others—10.72 (Noah); 11.29 (Noah), 51 (Hūd); 26.109 (Noah), 127 (Hūd), 145 (Ṣāliḥ), 164 (Lot), 180 (Shu'ayb); 36.21 (unnamed).

3 A liberal Muslim who accepts the story is 'Alī Dashtī, *Twenty-three Years*, tr. F. R. C. Bagley, London 1985, 31f.

4 See p.30 and n.25; also *EI*², art. (al-)Lāt (T. Fahd).

5 The Qur'ānic references will be found in Paret, *Kommentar*, on 7.184.

6 See *Bell's Introduction*, 127-35.

7 See Paret, *Kommentar*, on 4.101 and 6.110.

8 Further references in Paret, *Kommentar* on 10.65.

9 Ibn Hishām, 313f.

10 See Paret, *Kommentar*, on 17.76, with further references.

Index

(The Arabic article al-, an-, etc. is neglected in the alphabetical ordering.)

Aaron, 76, 100
'abd, 16, 56f., 101
'Abd-Allāh ibn-Ubayy, 25
'Abd-ad-Dār, 13
'Abd-al-Muṭṭalib, 48f.
Abraha, 15
Abraham, 17, 22, 24f., 37-9, 43, 58, 60, 75f., 80, 89
Abū-Bakr, 103, 106
Abū-Lahab, 103
Abū-Sufyān, 30, 89
Abū-Ṭālib, 23, 48f., 102f.
Abyssinia(ns), 15f., 36, 38f., 44, 88
'Ād, 49
Adam, 75, 91
'Ā'isha, 55
ajal, 26-8
Allāh (as high god), 31-6, 38f., 49, 59, 87-9, 92f.
amr, 50, 58, 62-4
angels, 30f., 33, 49, 57, 63, 67f., 77f., 85, 87, 90, 97
Anṣār, 20
awliyā', see: *walī*
āya, āyāt, 66, 70, 73, 79

Badr, 61
Baḥīrā, 48
banāt Allāh, 30, 87
bashīr, 72-4, 76
al-Bayḍāwī, 2, 6, 11, 15, 19, 78
Bell, Richard, 2-4, 57, 64, 68, 72, 77, 79f.
Bible, 44f., 52f., 59, 66
Blachère, R., 4, 14, 73, 82, 87, 93
Black Stone, 38
blood-money, 18
Book, the, 79f., 89, see also: *kitāb*
al-Bukhārī, 1
Byzantine(s), 13f., 17, 36, 38, 44

Christians, Christianity, 2, 13, 16, 36-8, 44-6, 48, 53, 56, 59, 64, 66, 88

dahr, 26f., 30
ḍalāl, *ḍāll*, 6, 49
Damascus, 14, 44
David, 52, 76
dhikr, *dhikrā*, 74f.
Dhū-Nuwās, 13
diya, 18

Elephant (expedition of), 15, 39
Emigrants, 20, 25, 101
Ezra ('Uzayr), 2, 45

fathers, 20-5

Gabriel, 54-6, 58, 62, 67, 77
Gaza, 44
Gentiles, 53
ghanī, 41-3
ghayb, 66
Grimme, H., 3, 55

Ḥadīth, 1, 65
ḥalīf, 15
ḥanīf, 37f., 58
Hāshim, 23, 48, 102f., 105
Heraclius, 13
Hijra, 20, 25, 54, 103, 105
ḥilm, 43f., 84
Hubal, 30, 39
Hūd, 75, 91, 99
hudā, 6
al-Ḥudaybiya, 41, 52, 61
Hypocrites, 17, 25

Iblīs, 91
Ibn-Ḥabīb, 38
Ibn-Hishām, 1, 25
Ibn-Isḥāq, 38
Ibn-Qutayba, 38
Idrīs, 75, 80
i'jāz, 65
intercession, 32-6, 78f., 89
Iraq, 13, 40
Isaac, 22, 75f.

Ishmael, 22, 75f., 80
Israel, Israelites, 17, 59, 75f., 79
Isrāfīl, 55, 58
istaghnā, 42f., 83

Jacob, 22, 75f.
Jalālayn, 2, 34
jam' (al-Qur'ān), 62, 70
jār, 15, 19
Jerusalem, 13
Jesus, 2, 36, 45f., 65, 75f.
Jews, 2, 13, 36-8, 44f., 53, 56, 59, 64, 66, 75, 88
jinn, 31, 65, 90f., 96, 103
Joseph, 65, 91
Judaism, 36, 44f.

Ka'ba, 31, 37-40, 73
Khadīja, 50
Khazraj, 25
kitāb, 27, 53, see also: Book

Lane, E. W., 25, 57, 74
al-Lāt, 29f., 86f., 91
Lot, 99, 105

Madā'in Ṣāliḥ, 14
majnūn, 96
māl, amwāl, 41-4
mala', 17, 23
Manāt, 29, 86f.
Ma'rib, 12
Mary, 2, 45, 80
mathānī, 79f.
mawlā, 16, 19, 27
Medina, 3, 15, 17, 20, 25, 36, 43f., 50, 52, 72, 78-80, 91, 101-6
Midian, 41
milla, 17, 37
Moses, 21, 23, 28, 53, 57, 59, 65f., 76, 80, 100, 104
mothers, 22f.
mudhakkir, 72, 74, 84
Muir, W., 3, 55
Mu'ta, 14

nabī, 72, 75-7
nadhīr, 72-4, 76
an-Nadr ibn-al-Ḥārith, 13
Najrān, 13
nasab, 15
naṣīr, naṣr, 19f., 89
naskh, 70
nawm, 60
New Testament, 45f., 65
Noah, 23f., 28f., 57, 64f., 75f., 99f.
Nöldeke, Th., 3f., 14, 57

Old Testament, 18, 45, 75

Paret, R., 2, 79
Persian(s), 13, 38
Pharaoh, 17, 76f., 83, 99f.
Pickthall, M., 2, 53
predestination, 21, 26-8
'protection', 15-20, 102-6, see also: *naṣīr*

qawm, 16f., 72
Quraysh, 16, 39, 73
Quṣayy, 17

ar-Raḥmān, 93
rasūl, 54f., 72, 76-9
retaliation, 18f.
revelation, see: *waḥy*
  manners of, 60-7
  occasions of, 2f.
rizq, 9, 26-8, 31, 89
Romans, 13
ru'ya, 60

ṣalāt, 59
Ṣāliḥ, 14, 23, 75, 99f., 104
Satan, 31, 70f., 92
sayyid, 17
Shahāda, 92f.
Shahid, I., 13
shar', shara'a, 64
Sheba, 12
  queen of, 17
shirk, 92, see also: *shurakā'*
Shu'ayb, 23, 43, 94, 99f., 102, 105
shurakā', 30, 33f., 89f.
ṣihr, 15
slaves, 16, 45
Solomon, 17, 76
South Arabia(n), 12, 29, 52
Spirit, the, 63f., 77
Syria, 13, 36, 39f., 48

aṭ-Ṭabarī, 2, 86
ṭaghā, 83f.
aṭ-Ṭā'if, 29, 50, 86, 103, 105

Ṭālūt (Saul), 42
tazakkī, 59f.
Teixidor, 38, 109 (n.30)
Thamūd, 14, 41, 76, 99
Time, 26, 30
Torrey, C. C., 40

Uḥud, 28, 30, 50, 87
ʿUmar, 103
umma, 16, 20, 72
ummī, ummiyyūn, 49, 51-3, 76
ʿUthmān, 62
al-ʿUzzā, 29f., 49, 86f., 91

Wadd, 29
waḥy, 1, 57-60, 62f.
walī, awliyā', 16, 19f., 24f., 32, 36, 89f.
Waraqa, 44, 52, 59
warner, see: *nadhīr, mudhakkir*

Yemen, 15, 39f., 44

Zacharias, 57, 65
zakāt, 49, 60, 79
az-Zamakhsharī, 2